FIVE IDEAS TO FIGHT FOR

'A powerful rallying cry for the creation of a civilised world made by the founding father of modern human rights in the UK – a hero of our times.'
Helena Kennedy QC

'Anthony Lester has throughout his life – and often far in advance of his times – been an eloquent fighter for freedom of speech, equality under the law, protection from official arbitrariness and much else besides. His views and actions – as lawyer, legislator and citizen – have often irked those in power but have conduced to justice, human dignity and a sense of reasonableness and decency in the world around him. In this book he combines legal and political argument with telling personal anecdote – and he does so with a most engaging combination of practicality and passion.'
Vikram Seth, author of *A Suitable Boy*

'The five ideas the great human rights lawyer, Anthony Lester, calls us to fight for are the foundations of liberty in the modern world. Today they are besieged by intolerance, cynicism and indifference.'
Shirley Williams

'All the forces that, for decades, abused the human rights of the thalidomide children, are on the rise again in an ugly xenophobic populism: those who have the loudest voices have the smallest vision. They must be repulsed and there is no better person to summon us to the ramparts than the author of this exciting book.'
Sir Harold Evans, editor-at-large for Thomson Reuters and former editor of *The Sunday Times*

'Anthony Lester has spent his life in the dedicated pursuit of freedom and justice, both as a lawyer and as a member of the House of Lords. We need to listen to his urgent case for upholding these core values and be inspired by the courage and passion with which he continues to fight for them.'
Mary Robinson, President of the Republic of Ireland, 1990–1997, and former UN High Commissioner for Human Rights

'Animated by the desire to protect fundamental human rights and freedoms in a long and distinguished career in law as a practitioner and lawmaker, Anthony Lester makes a passionate case for the defence of these rights – so hard won and so much under threat today.'
Southall Black Sisters

Five Ideas
to
Fight For

How Our Freedom
Is Under Threat and
Why It Matters

ANTHONY LESTER

ONEWORLD

A Oneworld Book

First published in North America, Great Britain and
Australia by Oneworld Publications, 2016

ISBN 978-1-78074-761-3
ISBN 978-1-78074-762-0 (eBook)

Typeset by Hewer Text UK Ltd, Edinburgh
Printed and bound in Great Britain by Clays Ltd, St Ives plc

Oneworld Publications
10 Bloomsbury Street
London WC1B 3SR
England

CONTENTS

For Katya, Gideon, Maya and Benjamin.

ACKNOWLEDGEMENTS

This book began three years ago prompted by Zoe McCallum, a postgraduate working for the Bill of Rights Commission. I needed to be persuaded because there are too many self-serving political memoirs and lawyers' casebooks, and I did not want to add to them. But Zoe prevailed and has collaborated in drafting and editing a book about the ideas for which I have fought. She is an exceptional young writer and political advocate (soon to be at the Bar).

My wife Katya patiently supported my work and writing and my tilting at windmills. Without her loving support I would have achieved little. Our son Gideon, who escaped law for theatre in the USA, suggested the title and shaped the work. Our daughter Maya, a far better barrister than me, enriched my understanding of the law and beyond.

Thanks to the generosity of David Sainsbury's Gatsby Charitable Foundation, the Sigrid Rausing Trust and the Open Society Institute, I have had crucial back up for my political office, the Odysseus Trust. Zoe McCallum, Caroline Baker, Emma Fenelon and Clare Duffy helped me to prepare the book.

They are the most recent in a long line of brilliant young women and men who have collaborated in my political work.

My literary agent, Zoë Pagnamenta, led me to my publisher, Oneworld, owned by its founders, Novin Doostdar and Juliet Mabey. It has made all the difference to have the backing of a nimble and public-spirited publisher. Unlike so many in the international book trade these days, Oneworld is not owned by a conglomerate and publishes not to make huge profits but to support interesting works. They and their editors, first Mike Harpley and more recently Sam Carter, have helped me to cut and polish and refine. I am also grateful to their publicity director Margot Weale, and Becky Kraemer who acts for Oneworld in the USA.

Many others have read draft chapters and given their feedback. With apologies to those inadvertently omitted, I am grateful to Gloria Abdullah, David Anderson, Lisa Appignanesi, Jo Ashby, Mairead and Tony Barry, Janet Benshoof, Jonathan Self, Roger Berry, Tim Colbourne, Sandy Coliver, Jonathan Cooper, Jill Davidson, Charlotte Dewar, Harry Evans, Margaret Ferguson, Melanie Field, Maurice Frankel, Jo Glanville, Jim Goldston, Martine Croxall, Beth Hallinan, Rebecca Hilsenrath, Susan Hitch, Greg Jones, Kate Jones, Jeffrey Jowell, Jocelyn Keith, Ken Keith, Gail Kent, Amanda Lamugisha, Anne Lapping, Brian Lapping, Mick Levens, Teo Soh Lung, Sujata Manohar, Monica McWilliams, Rose Mulcahy, Anthony Neoh, Anthony and Julia Neuberger, Angelika Nussberger, Michael O'Boyle, Kate O'Regan, Simon and Louise Palmer, David Pannick, Kathy W. Pollak, Dinah Rose, Khatun Sapnara, Pia Sarma, Katherine Schofield, Stephen Sedley, Jill Silverman van Coenegrachts, Audrey Simpson, Soli Sorabjee, David Stephen, Chris Stone and Frederick Wilmot-Smith.

I of course take full responsibility for the contents of the book, and for errors of fact and judgement.

NO TIME FOR APATHY

This book charts the ways that ideas about human rights, equality, free speech, privacy and the rule of law have evolved over the last sixty years. It explains why they matter, how well they are protected, and how they are threatened. It describes what has been achieved, how it happened, and what we need to fight for now. There is never a time for apathy, especially now.

This is not an autobiography, though some account of my life is given where relevant. It is not a lawyer's casebook, though cases I have argued are discussed where they have inspired reforms. It is not a political memoir, though it is highly political. It is not a scholarly work, but rather an overview of practical change in the five fields, drawing on my experience as a barrister, parliamentarian and campaigner – at home and abroad.

I want to show that it is possible to bring about change and to encourage active engagement. The British political system has been decaying for decades and is falling apart. The main parties are split into hostile factions. They play clumsy games with our fragile constitution, like children playing with boxes of matches. The American diplomat Dean Acheson once observed that

Britain had lost an empire but not yet found a place in the world. That remains true. Britain is only half in Europe, a semi-detached and grumpy member punching below its weight and size. Foreign invasions, terrorism and mass migration have bred fear and insecurity, conditions easily exploited by extremists.

Our increasingly disunited kingdom is threatened by powerful forces of nationalism – pressure exerted by those who would quit the European Union or the United Kingdom or both, and from those who would impose their values and beliefs on the rest of us. This threatens our secular tradition. There is a risk that our governors may sleepwalk the UK into leaving the European Union, and that Scotland may leave the rest of the UK, and that Northern Ireland will remain politically polarised.

Disintegration of the UK and disengagement from Europe would weaken our capacity to tackle the problems that cannot be solved by a single country – perplexing problems of corruption, inequality between rich and poor, racism, terrorism, xenophobia, the misuse of religion as a weapon of mass destruction, and the devastation of the global ecosystem.

The Astronomer Royal, Martin Rees, has warned that we are 'destroying the book of life before we have read it'. The pressures of a growing human population and economy, on land and on water, are already high and we have a responsibility 'to our children, to the poorest, to steward the diversity and richness of life on earth'.[1] Working across Europe and beyond it, we must also tackle world hunger, disease and over-population; the effects of wars that have destroyed stable societies and resulted in millions of refugees; terrorism, racism and political extremism.

---

1 'Scientists and politicians alike must rally to protect life on earth', *Financial Times*, 6 September 2015.

This is the worrisome context in which the book explores the five ideas I have chosen to fight for. They reflect my practical experience and personal choices. They are not presented as a hierarchy of greater and lesser importance. The ideas are inter-dependent but each is looked at separately. Each has a particular history and its own dilemmas and puzzles. Each is under threat.

Do we really know why we are the way we are? Short of consulting a psychiatrist, I cannot be sure why I have spent my adult life fighting for these ideas. It had to do with my upbring-ing by Jewish parents whose European relatives had been murdered in the Holocaust and who sympathised with disad-vantaged people. It had to do with my education at a liberal school – Asquith's City of London School – in the 1950s, and with feeling the pinpricks of English anti-Semitism during National Service. It had to do with what I learned about politics when I studied history at Cambridge (discussed in the 'Equality' chapter).

When I left Cambridge in 1960, I had been put off a legal career by the austere diet of English law on which I had been fed. The unwritten common law was the staple curriculum for law undergraduates. Acts of Parliament were treated as unfit for university study. One ancient law professor from my college lamented the fact that industrial law and family law were enter-ing the syllabus even though they sprang from statutes.

I learned about the legal rules governing contracts, torts (civil wrongs) and crime but little attention was paid to law in context. Public law was undeveloped. My mentors, like the judges at that time, were uncritical of the way that state powers were used. Written constitutions were regarded with disdain as suitable only for less mature societies than ours. There was no developed equality or human rights law. English judges, sitting in the Judicial Committee of the Privy Council in appeals from the

3

former Empire, gave judgments condoning racial discrimination in Africa and Canada.

In 1962, I came back from the United States reluctantly, to a country whose rulers were depressingly complacent. At Harvard Law School I had learned the benefits and burdens of a written constitution and Bill of Rights. I had seen from abroad the flaws in the English legal system, which was narrowly legalistic and ethically aimless – without a compass to steer by. In those days, our most senior judges, the Law Lords, had denied themselves the power to overrule a previous judgment even if it was wrong.

I went back to the States for Amnesty International during what became known as the long hot summer of 1964. I was tasked to report on racial justice in the Deep South. It was a transforming experience. When I returned home and began to practise at the Bar in 1965 I was determined to use what I had learned and seen to protect human rights. I was uncomfortable in the snobbish, male-dominated, racist and arrogant world of the English Bar in those far-off days. I was initially refused a tenancy in my chambers on the ground that I was too political – too close to politics and the press. At that time I regarded the American system of government under law as vastly superior to ours.[2]

But the spirit of the age was beginning to change. It was reflected in the work of a new breed of legal scholars who were

---

2 I no longer think so. American judges are politically appointed or elected. Elections are dominated by wealth and the electoral machinery is wide open to corruption. The politically polarised US Congress filibusters obstruct much needed reforms on healthcare, gun control and other important topics. Public figures are defamed by wickedly untrue libels by Fox News and other media. Racism persists in criminal justice and prisons, and the death penalty is still lawful.

internationally minded. They understood the need for stronger safeguards against the misuse of the powers of the state. In 1959, Stanley de Smith had published his seminal work *Judicial Review of Administrative Action*. In 1961, after I had left Cambridge, H.R.W. Wade, my former mentor in property law, published *Administrative Law*. In 1963, Harry Street published *Freedom, The Individual and the Law*, the first survey of civil liberties in Britain. A year later, de Smith published *The New Commonwealth and its Constitutions*.

These oracles encouraged me to hope that a change of government to Labour would be infused with this new spirit. I was sadly mistaken. In 1963, Gerald Gardiner, soon to become Lord Chancellor in Harold Wilson's Labour government, published a book of collected essays with Andrew Martin, soon to become a member of the Law Commission. It was entitled *Law Reform Now*. Many of its proposals were progressive but the book said nothing about the need to protect fundamental human rights. At a time when the judges were executive-minded and timorous in challenging government decisions, one essay on administrative law in the book even rebuked judges for being over-enthusiastic in using their powers of judicial review.[3]

In 1966, the Wilson government allowed cases against the UK to be taken to the European Court of Human Rights in Strasbourg. But it shied away from making rights enshrined in the European Convention on Human Rights part of domestic law, or strengthening the courts' ability to curb abuses of power. A year later I argued the first British case to the European Commission of Human Rights on behalf of a Pakistani mill

---

3 *Law Reform Now* (London: V. Gollancz Ltd, 1963), p. 52. The essay was presumably written by John Griffiths, a fierce left-wing critic of the judiciary for what he regarded as its reactionary decisions.

worker from Bradford and his young son, who had been refused permission to join him in the UK. We won the argument and the government undertook to allow the boy to join his father. It also promised to introduce an immigration appeal system – the first of its kind.[4] That made me appreciate that the European Convention system could provide remedies where there were none in our courts.

The following year, in 1968, Harold Wilson's Labour government rushed an emergency Bill through Parliament in three days and nights. It took away the right of British Asians from East Africa to enter and live in the UK. It was racist, and in breach of a pledge by a previous British government – that if East Africa's newly independent governments expelled British Asians, they would retain the right to settle in the UK. But because the Westminster Parliament is supreme and the courts cannot strike down Acts of Parliament, the only way of challenging the law was to complain to the European Commission of Human Rights in Strasbourg. That seemed to me to be absurd. The Commission was a vital long stop – but we needed effective remedies for violations in our own courts.

In November 1968, I gave a Fabian lecture advocating a Bill of Rights built on the European Convention on Human Rights. It would put a protective fence around fundamental rights and freedoms.[5] There were plenty of American but few British thinkers that I could rely on to support my argument. In 1859, J.S. Mill had warned in his essay *On Liberty* against populism becoming a weapon of arbitrary power – the 'tyranny of the majority'. Eight decades later, in 1939, H.G. Wells had championed the

---

4 *Alam and Khan v United Kingdom* Application 2991/66 (1967).
5 *Democracy and Individual Rights*, Fabian Society Tract 390 (London: Fabian Society, 1969).

need for an international declaration of human rights. In 1945, Hersch Lauterpacht (later to become the British judge on the International Court of Justice) published his seminal work *An International Bill for the Rights of Man*, which faced up to the English dogma of parliamentary sovereignty. Harold Laski, influenced by his contact with the United States, observed in 1948 that the real value of a Bill of Rights was to act 'as a rallying-point in the State for all who care deeply for the ideals of freedom'.[6]

The *New York Times* chief London correspondent, Anthony Lewis, attended my lecture. He agreed with the need for a modern British Bill of Rights based on the Convention but doubted it would ever come to pass. Most British thinkers fifty years ago regarded the idea of fundamental rights with disdain – suitable for the United States or Napoleon's Europe or newly independent Commonwealth countries, but not for the United Kingdom. Ivor Jennings, a leading British constitutional scholar and grand poo-bah of his day, regarded India's written constitution with disdain. In 1954, Herbert Morrison, former Deputy Prime Minister, published *Government and Parliament*, glorifying the status quo without any mention of abuses of power or the rights of the individual. In 1957, Prime Minister Harold Macmillan told his fellow Conservatives that the British had 'never had it so good'.

In several cases I tried to persuade our judges to take human rights more seriously, quoting American and European analogies. My successes were few. I found that I was able to achieve more in two years as special adviser to Roy Jenkins at the Home Office – in 1974–76 – than in ten years at the Bar. We shaped sex

---

6 Harold Laski, *Liberty and the Modern State* (London: George Allen & Unwin Ltd, 1948), p. 65.

and race discrimination laws and advanced the case for a British Bill of Rights.

When I returned reluctantly to the Bar in 1976 I no longer had a practice in commercial law. But I developed a practice in what is now known as public law – the judicial review of the actions of public bodies to ensure they act lawfully, rationally and fairly. I acted as well in cases on equality, free speech, privacy and other human rights, making submissions before a new generation of judges whose values were very different from those of their predecessors.

Meanwhile, the Labour Party turned against Europe and liberalism and became dominated by trade union corporatism. My political life declined after I was rejected as a parliamentary Labour candidate whose views were out of favour. When the Gang of Four[7] broke with Labour and set up the Social Democratic Party I went with them, and later joined the merged Liberal Democrats. During that time my barristers' chambers were enriched by a new generation of women and men – better educated than we had been and keen to take on public interest cases.

There were clear limits to what could be achieved using the judicial process. In 1993, I turned down the offer of a High Court judgeship for which I was ill suited. Thanks to Paddy Ashdown, then leader of the Liberal Democrats, I became a member of the House of Lords instead, focusing on the constitutional and human rights issues that I cherish.

Peers are unelected and independent-minded – counter-majoritarian and sometimes in the vanguard of ground-breaking reform. About a fifth of the House of Lords are not appointed by the political parties. That secures our independence. Because of

---

7 Roy Jenkins, Shirley Williams, Bill Rodgers and David Owen.

them, the government does not have a commanding majority and can be defeated by cross-party alliances. We have much more time than members of the Commons to debate and introduce reforming Bills. And among the politicians of yesteryear are experts in many fields, including law and government, academia and the professions.

For all but the five years of coalition government, I have sat on the opposition benches under Conservative and Labour governments, working with colleagues from all parties and none, as well as civil society. My maiden speech was about the need for better human rights protection. I used public lectures and questions to ministers and Private Members' Bills to achieve reforms – Bills on human rights, equality, civil partnership, forced marriage, constitutional reform and defamation.

When Gordon Brown replaced Tony Blair as Prime Minister in 2007 he made a powerful statement on the case for constitutional reform. I was invited informally to rejoin the Labour Party and become a minister. When I declined I was invited to become an unpaid independent adviser to the Lord Chancellor, Jack Straw, as what became known as a 'goat' – a reference to a 'government of all the talents'. My experience as a tethered goat inside Gordon Brown's big tent was an exercise in futility. I resigned after fifteen months when it became plain that Gordon Brown, Jack Straw and their colleagues had wasted the opportunity of a generation for constitutional reform.[8]

There was one redeeming achievement by the Brown government before it lost power. Under Harriet Harman's determined leadership, what became the Equality Act 2010 was successfully navigated. It became law on the eve of the General Election on 6

---

8 Anthony Lester, 'My misery as a tethered goat in Gordon Brown's big tent', *Guardian*, 27 July 2009.

May 2010. It was modelled on my Private Member's Equality Bill, introduced seven years before, and had crucial support from the Liberal Democrats.

The five years in coalition with the Conservatives were painful because we Lib Dems had to support measures with which we strongly disagreed. An embarrassing example of excessive loyalty arose during the passage of the Public Bodies Bill designed to axe or merge many 'quangos'.[9] The former Lord Chief Justice, Lord Woolf, had accused ministers of treating some of the quangos in a cavalier fashion. So I introduced an amendment restricting the way ministers could use their new powers by forcing them to ensure that they respected judicial independence and human rights.

The government was vigorously opposed to my amendment. When I was strong-armed I tried to withdraw it – but the cross-benches objected and my amendment was passed.[10] From a surfeit of loyalty I voted idiotically against my own amendment. I am much happier to be back in opposition, no longer having to perform political contortions to vote for unconscionable proposals.

The Liberal Democrats suffered a devastating defeat in the 2015 General Election, but I do not believe that the British people rejected liberalism. The current government wants to suppress extremist activity, and the Prime Minister and Home Secretary define extremism as 'vocal or active opposition to fundamental British values'. Those surely are the values of a liberal society that include freedom for political dissent and respect for human rights and the rule of law (see the 'Free Speech' chapter).

---

9 Quasi-autonomous non-governmental organisations.
10 HL Deb 23 November 2010, vol. 722, cols. 1010–1041.

Those fundamental values are threatened not only by terrorists but by the state and its agents and populist politicians. Human rights are under threat at home and abroad. So is the international reputation of the UK as a country that respects the European rule of law. David Cameron's government was elected with a pledge to tear up the Human Rights Act, replacing it with a 'British Bill of Rights and Responsibilities'. It is not likely to give greater protection to our rights and freedoms than what we have now. The European Court of Human Rights is under attack by ministers for having supposedly undermined the sovereignty of the Westminster Parliament.

Successive governments have continued to flout the Strasbourg Court's judgments requiring at least some convicted prisoners to be entitled to vote in parliamentary elections. That violates our international legal obligations. It sets a shameful example for pseudo-democracies when they too violate human rights.

I hope that this book will encourage readers to fight for the country we love – and for a more open, democratic society based on equal justice under the rule of law. Each chapter highlights the history, the threats we face and the challenges to human rights, equality, free speech, privacy and the rule of law.

1

HUMAN RIGHTS

'Power is delightful and absolute power is absolutely delightful.'
Notice on a Home Office immigration official's desk in the 1960s

'For too long we have been a passively tolerant society, saying to our citizens "as long as you obey the law, we will leave you alone".'
David Cameron (13 May 2015)

The way we protect human rights is under sustained attack. Politicians and sections of the press peddle lies and distortions about the European Convention on Human Rights, the Strasbourg Court and the Human Rights Act. They allege that the system distorts justice, preventing evil people from getting their just deserts. They complain that it hampers governments in tackling terrorism and serious crime. They decry rulings preventing deportation to a country where there is a risk of torture or the death penalty. They object when a court rules that bed and breakfast owners must not refuse to accommodate a gay couple. They blame the Human Rights Act when our soldiers are made to account for complicity in torture. They accuse the Strasbourg Court of undermining democracy by being too activist and overriding our sovereign Parliament.

The phrase 'human rights' has become a buzzword used to attack judges and the rule of law here and in Europe. It has weakened public confidence in the system that protects our basic rights and freedoms – as well as public confidence in our judges, who cannot answer back.

Journalists and the public need human rights law to protect a free press. Newspapers rely on the Convention to protect free speech, but many editors and their owners do not accept that they must respect the human rights of those whose private lives they expose for commercial gain. That is one reason why the public is fed a diet of half-truths and downright lies about the so-called 'threats' to our way of life. Story after story is run each week attacking what they describe as 'this human rights farce',[1] calling the Human Rights Act a 'gift to our enemies',[2] and demanding that the government ignore the rulings of 'this foreign court'.[3] That makes good

---

1 E.g. 'New human rights farce as police are afraid to release crooks' mugshots', *Mail on Sunday*, 14 July 2014; 'Criminal freed in human rights farce put teacher in fear', *Daily Mail*, 30 May 2011; 'This human rights farce', *Daily Mail*, 25 May 2007; 'May: I will kick foreign lags out: Home Sec vows to end human rights farce', *Sun*, 3 October 2011; 'Human rights "farce": Exclusive home office fury after drug dealer immigrant wins right to stay in UK because of his "family life" ', *Sunday Telegraph*, 28 April 2013; 'Human rights "farce" let 300 criminals stay in UK', *Express*, 3 September 2013; 'Human rights "farce" over migrant checks', *Express*, 3 August 2013.

2 'Human Rights Act is a gift to our enemies', *Daily Mail*, 8 November 2013.

3 E.g. 'The European Court of Human Rights is an absurd yoke around Britain's neck', *Telegraph*, 22 May 2012; 'Vote is criminal', *Sun*, 19 January

copy and boosts sales, as does salacious gossip about the private lives of public figures. But it undermines public confidence in the very system that protects their and their readers' free expression.

Populist ministers are also to blame. In September 2013, the Home Secretary, Theresa May, voiced her frustration at her inability to deport the radical cleric Abu Qatada to Jordan because of the risk that evidence gained through torture might be used against him in a trial there. She found it ridiculous that the government should have 'to go to such lengths to get rid of dangerous foreigners'. That is why, she explained, 'the next Conservative manifesto will promise to scrap the Human Rights Act . . . It's why the Conservative position is clear – if leaving the European Convention is what it takes to fix our human rights laws, that is what we should do'.[4]

The then Lord Chancellor, Chris Grayling, also declared his hostility to the Act and the Strasbourg Court. Kenneth Clarke and Dominic Grieve were the only two Conservative ministers within the coalition to stand up publicly for the European rule of law. Clarke retired and Grieve was removed from office shortly afterwards.

It was not ever thus. After the Second World War, the Conservative Party led the way under Winston Churchill and David Maxwell Fyfe in creating the Convention system. Yet now the Cameron government wants to tear up the Human Rights Act to replace it with a 'British Bill of Rights'. It invokes the

---

2011; 'It would make a mockery of justice but foreign judges could rule that Britain's mass murderers have a human right to be set free', *Daily Mail*, 27 November 2012.
4 'Conservatives promise to scrap Human Rights Act after next election', *Guardian*, 30 September 2013.

Conservative election manifesto to justify its threatened measures. At first it hinted at the possibility of withdrawing altogether from the Convention and the institutions which oversee it, the European Court of Human Rights and the Council of Europe. It then rowed back from that position. The Prime Minister, Justice Minister, Home Secretary and their supporters in Parliament are populists, driven by the wish to appease anti-European MPs in the Commons and to be rid of Strasbourg Court rulings with which they disagree. They have amended the Ministerial Code to delete the duty to comply with international law and treaty obligations.

Ministers want to be free to send away a suspected terrorist even to a country where he would risk torture or face the death penalty. They would like Parliament to limit the courts' powers to review the legality of what they can and cannot do. They would like to give more power to themselves in Parliament to overrule judgments that they dislike. If we do not succeed in defending the way we protect human rights, five decades of hard-fought progress will be lost.

What are human rights?

We must strive to protect the basic rights we all enjoy because of our shared humanity. They include the right to life, the right not to be tortured or subjected to inhuman or degrading treatment or punishment, the right not to be enslaved, the right to a fair trial, to freedom of thought, conscience and religion, to freedom of expression, to respect for private and family life, the right to marry, the right to private property, to education, to take part in free and secret elections, and to enjoy these rights without discrimination. They are the bedrock of a democracy based on the rule of law and our common humanity and dignity. They call for special protection against undue interference and abuse whether by elected politicians or public officials.

Human rights are not the gift of governments. They are our birthright. Some believe human rights are part of natural law and religious teachings; for others they are fruits of the eighteenth-century Enlightenment; for pragmatists they are the basic freedoms of the individual. Philosophers and theologians reflect about origins and sources of fundamental rights. I am neither a philosopher nor a theologian. What matters to me is whether they are observed in practice and whether there are effective remedies for victims when they are breached.

Some rights are suitable to be enforced by judges. Others should be put into effect by the government. It is the responsibility of the political branches to secure and protect economic, social and cultural rights. Judges have no competence or expertise to decide how to create a health service, or tackle poverty, or make the trains run on time. It is not the judges' function to solve political problems or to consult the public about them. Judges have no mandate to make law and must take care to keep off the political grass when deciding how to balance individual rights and the public interest.

It is only rarely, when the democratically elected arms of the state have failed completely to fulfil their obligations to protect economic, social and cultural rights, that the courts may intervene, for example, to prevent starvation or to halt discrimination in providing healthcare. If the courts attempted to impose an economic theory or a political ideology, they would undermine both their legitimacy and public confidence in the administration of justice.

Origins of the European system

The European Convention on Human Rights came into force in 1953. The barbarous atrocities of the Second World War – the mass extermination of millions of Jews, gypsies, gay men and the disabled, mass torture, discrimination and pillage – enabled the newly born Council of Europe to muster enough political will to create the Convention in the late 1940s. Without Hitler's Nazi Reich, there would have been no Convention – no moral compass to guide governments and to protect the governed through European and national laws.

The Council of Europe's founders understood the need to forge a new international system of human rights protection that transcended political and legal frontiers. They sought to guard against the rise of new dictatorships, to reduce the risk of relapse into another disastrous European war, and to provide a beacon of hope for the peoples of Central and Eastern Europe living under the yoke of totalitarian Soviet regimes. They were determined never again to permit state sovereignty to shield the perpetrators of crimes against humanity from international liability; never again to allow governments to hide with impunity behind the traditional argument that what a state does to its own citizens or to outsiders is its business and beyond the reach of international law.

The Strasbourg system was a revolutionary initiative. For the first time, individual men and women would be able to enforce their rights against their own governments before an international court, the European Court of Human Rights. British politicians and lawyers made key contributions to the final wording of the Convention. They were determined that it would reflect the values that our country had fought to preserve in our battle against Hitler. The final version is as British as roast beef and Yorkshire pudding.

When the Convention was being prepared, in 1949, Clement Attlee's Labour government had deep reservations about it. The Cabinet papers reveal that Lord Chancellor Jowett opposed the creation of a supranational court. The Chancellor of the Exchequer, Stafford Cripps, believed the Convention was inconsistent with a planned economy. The Attorney General, Hartley Shawcross, regarded the possibility of UK citizens lodging complaints against their government in Strasbourg as 'wholly opposed to the theory of responsible government'.[5]

Like David Cameron's government today, the Attlee government saw itself as protecting the integrity of the British constitution and the judicial system against subversive European influence. But the Foreign Secretary, Ernest Bevin, argued that the European movement could not be held back and that the UK was in danger of being politically isolated. He persuaded the Cabinet to agree to ratification. It did so reluctantly, on condition that the UK would not allow individuals to take a case against the state to Strasbourg. In those days the system allowed governments to deny individuals the right to bring a case.

On 8 March 1951, the UK became the first among the nineteen founding Council of Europe states to ratify the Convention. Lord McNair, a British scholar of international law, became the first President of the European Court of Human Rights, in 1959. Successive governments continued to refuse

---

5 Letter of 4 October 1950, from the Right Honourable Sir Hartley Shawcross QC MP, LCO 2/5570.

the right to complain against the UK to the European Commission and Court of Human Rights or to make the Convention rights part of British law; so the Convention had no practical value to victims in the UK.

It was Harold Wilson's Labour government that accepted the right of individual petition in January 1966. The decision was taken at a time when the Strasbourg Court had decided only one case. There was no formal decision by the Cabinet and no parliamentary debate. Yet the consequences were far-reaching. It meant that individuals could challenge Acts of Parliament and judgments of our highest courts for violating Convention rights.

After the collapse of the Soviet Empire in 1989, membership of the Convention rapidly enlarged to include formerly totalitarian states. Today, the Convention binds forty-seven members of the Council of Europe. It requires each of them to give effective remedies in their national systems for breaches of the Convention rights and obliges them to comply with the Court's final rulings against them, however much they disagree. It gives – or is supposed to give – equal protection to some 820 million citizens of Europe, as well as non-citizens, from Ireland in the West to Azerbaijan in the East, from Russia in the North to Greece in the South.

Because it is an international court of last resort and not a court of appeal, the Strasbourg Court does not take the place of the national authorities. It takes on a case only when the national system fails to provide an effective remedy for a violation of a Convention right. It grants governments a margin of appreciation, aware that contracting states have a better knowledge of their own political, social and cultural traditions than a European Court. When it finds a violation, the Court recognises that it is for the state concerned to choose how to give effect to its ruling.

In other words, the Court is cautious not to trespass into the political arena.

The prime responsibility for securing the Convention rights is at national and not at European level. But it is a convenient fiction for governments and European bureaucrats to suppose that the Convention is properly observed across Europe. And it is remote from what happens in practice. Few countries have courts that are really independent, decide cases impartially and respect human rights, however unpopular or inconvenient the decision may be to a citizen, the public or the state. The worst repeat offenders are Turkey, Italy, Russia, Romania and Ukraine.[6] The UK continues to flout binding judgments requiring at least some convicted prisoners to be allowed to vote in parliamentary elections.[7]

---

6 Turkey is the most prolific violator of the Convention and has been a party in 18% of all judgments finding at least one violation of the Convention between 1949 and 2014. Turkey most frequently violates the right to liberty and security (Article 5), the right to a fair trial within a reasonable time (Article 6) and the protection of property (Protocol 1 – Article 1). Italy is the second most frequent violator of the Convention. Between 1949 and 2014, 68% of cases finding a violation by Italy involved Article 6(1), due to the lengthy delays in the Italian justice system. Russia is the most prolific violator of the right of life and the prohibition of torture. Judgments against Russia comprise 56% and 45% respectively of all the Article 2 and Article 3 violations found by the Court. Two former Soviet states rank fourth and fifth. Romania has frequently violated the protection of property (Protocol 1 – Article 1). Ukraine has frequently been found in breach of the right to a fair trial (Article 6) and the protection of property (Protocol 1 – Article 1).

7 *Hirst v United Kingdom* (No. 2) [2005] ECHR 681. The UK has been repeatedly criticised by the Committee of Ministers of the Council of Europe for flouting the Court's rulings, while the Russian Federation has indicated its interest in following the British example.

English opposition to bringing rights home

It took decades to win the right to complain to our *own* courts about violations of their Convention rights. Although from 1966, alleged victims of UK violations could seek redress in Strasbourg after the damage had been done, they could not rely directly on their Convention rights in UK courts. While the Convention was not part of our law, ministers, politicians and public authorities could not be called to account in our courts for decisions that were incompatible with it.

There was strong resistance among English politicians and civil servants to the idea of giving the Convention rights direct effect in UK law. When I suggested the idea in a public lecture in 1968, it was greeted with incredulity by almost everyone. In 1998, we won the Human Rights Act at last. We now rely upon the Act, on the Strasbourg Court and our own courts (as well as the common law) as our legal bulwark against the abuse of power by the state and its agents.

Hostility to judicial enforcement of fundamental rights is deeply rooted in history. Since the seventeenth century, the UK has been governed by a peculiarly English constitutional principle: the absolute sovereignty of Parliament. Under the English system a governing party with a majority in the Commons can make or unmake any law without the restraint of a supreme law of the constitution. The Dentists Act could in theory repeal the Act of Union 1707 with Scotland or the Scotland Act 1998, or the Bill of Rights 1689. That is because our courts treated all Acts of Parliament as equal and equally able to be trumped by a future Act of a future Parliament.

That is not the position in the rest of Europe or the rest of the democratic Commonwealth, apart from New Zealand. Their written constitutions require their legislatures to use their powers in a way that is compatible with their Bills of Rights, and that is what the Human Rights Act now does in a more nuanced way.

Fifty years ago, we had no modern system of public law and no Human Rights Act. There was nothing our courts could do to protect us from a Parliament that abused its powers. Francis Bacon, the seventeenth-century Lord Chancellor, warned judges to remember that their office is 'to interpret law, and not to make law, or give law'. His essay ended: 'let them be lions, but yet lions under the throne; being circumspect that they do not check or oppose any points of sovereignty'.[8] Our judges have been careful to obey the warning, but some judges have cautioned that they could one day be provoked to refuse to recognise the legitimacy of an arbitrary Act of Parliament.[9] If that were to happen, there would be a major constitutional crisis.

Each society has its own pathology of human rights violations. Fifty years ago, most British human rights problems stemmed from a lack of judicial control of powers delegated by Parliament to ministers and public officials. The conventional wisdom was that the gentlemen in Whitehall knew best, and that they and their ministers could be trusted to act fairly and reasonably without the need for judges to look over their shoulders. Civil servants would use their benevolent wisdom in acting as guardians of the public interest. Powers would be protected

---

8 Francis Bacon, 'Of Judicature', in *The Essays* (London: Macmillan and Co, 1902), p. 136.
9 E.g. Sir John Laws, 'Law and Democracy', (1995) *Public Law* 72; *Jackson v Attorney General* [2005] UKHL 56 §102; Lord Woolf, 'Droit Public – English Style', (1995) *Public Law* 57.

from misuse by ministers' sense of fair play. If a politician erred, the free press would expose the wrongdoing. The remedy would be achieved through politics and publicity, not the courts. If powers were abused, the rascals would be booted out at the next election.

That conventional wisdom has much in its favour. One virtue of our unwritten constitution is that it is flexible. It can be changed easily to meet current needs and values. Change comes from legislation when governments have the necessary political will and skill. It comes from court rulings that gradually clarify and develop the law. Another advantage of parliamentary supremacy is that it does not give exclusive responsibility to judges to protect human rights. It recognises the crucial role of the elected branches of government. It also avoids the trap of legalism – that is, strict obedience to the letter rather than the spirit of the law.

But our system has serious disadvantages too. Most modern democracies protect their civic values in their written constitutions as well as in ordinary laws. In the UK, we do not have a codified constitution expressing our core civic values. Our system is based on the supremacy of the Westminster Parliament, the rule of law and a political culture that cherishes individual liberty. We have important Acts of Parliament defining and protecting some of our basic rights – the Equality Acts, the Freedom of Information Act and the Representation of the People Act, for example. But unlike France, Germany, Italy, Canada, India, South Africa or the United States, we have no supreme constitution that proclaims our political and legal values, subject to alteration only by special procedures.

A government with a commanding majority in the House of Commons enjoys much greater power than most other democracies, and can trump the unelected House of Lords. That is why a former Lord Chancellor, Lord Hailsham of St Marylebone, described our system as an 'elected dictatorship'. In theory, there is nothing in law that would prevent a future Parliament from abolishing the courts, unless the courts themselves were to decide not to recognise what Parliament had done because it violated the rule of law and the basic structure of our (unwritten) constitution.

In the 1960s, UK governments exported the Convention wholesale to many countries of its former Empire. The Convention rights were codified in independence constitutions in Commonwealth Africa, Asia and the Caribbean. But UK governments still refused to make those rights directly enforceable in our own courts. It was fine to bridle the powers of Commonwealth governments and legislatures but not the Crown in Parliament.

A cynic might describe opposition to a modern Bill of Rights as based on the self-interest of bureaucrats for whom power is delightful and absolute power absolutely delightful.[10] Ministers and their civil servants of that age enjoyed being able to use their powers without the inconvenience of judges looking over their shoulders and applying a code of human rights. There was much to be said in favour of their view that a culture of liberty matters more than a hundred paper constitutions. Law is not a panacea. A charter of human rights can only work if it commands public

---

10 The late Sir Bob Hepple has recalled that he saw this displayed on a Home Office immigration officer's desk when he escaped to the UK from South Africa. *Young Man with a Red Tie: A Memoir of Mandela and the Failed Revolution, 1960–63* (South Africa: Jacana Media Ltd, 2013).

confidence and is rooted in a culture of respect for it. The written constitutions of Soviet countries were full of statements of rights and freedoms, but they were meaningless in practice.

The Whitehall mandarins who were so hostile to a Bill of Rights saw themselves as independent Platonic guardians of the national interest, maintaining the integrity of government from London across the realm. They believed that the benevolent discretion of the administrator is preferable to lawyers' legalisms and an inflexible codified constitution. They considered themselves better able to understand the needs of government and the governed than judges remote in their ivory towers. They worried that a concern for individual rights would be at the expense of the interests of the community. They feared that a rights-based approach would undermine our parliamentary system. They worried that the inevitably vague language of a Bill of Rights would give too much power to unelected judges to make law – disguising it as interpretation.

These objections need to be taken seriously. But they do not justify root and branch opposition to a Human Rights Act, European oversight or a written constitution protecting human rights. The plight of vulnerable minorities in the UK thirty years before the Human Rights Act shows how much we need the oversight of the Convention system.

The Convention and the Strasbourg Court protected the right of gay people to love each other at a time when homosexual love was criminalised in the UK. In 1983, Strasbourg ruled that the very existence of the criminal offence caused fear and suffering and violated the right to a private life[11] – and later, in

---

11 *Dudgeon v United Kingdom* (1983) 5 EHRR 573.

2000, that a blanket ban on gay men and women serving in the armed forces breached the Convention.[12]

The Convention system provided redress to children in the 1980s and 1990s, when UK law still permitted corporal punishment in schools[13] and still allowed a stepfather to beat his stepson with impunity.[14] It protected parents when their local authority banned them from seeing their children without giving them a means to question the decision or argue against it.[15]

The Convention protected the right to privacy before it was recognised as part of UK law. The Strasbourg Court ruled that police could not tap telephones unless Parliament enacted a law specifically authorising them to do so.[16] It found against the authorities for deporting vulnerable people to countries where they faced a risk of torture or inhumane treatment.[17] It decided that a worker claiming unfair dismissal from his job had a right to have his case determined by the courts within a reasonable time.[18]

In the years before UK courts recognised a common law constitutional right to free speech, the Strasbourg Court came

---

12 *Smith and Grady v United Kingdom* (2000) 29 EHRR 493 (also see the 'Equality' chapter).

13 *Tyrer v United Kingdom* (1979–80) 2 EHRR 1.

14 *A v United Kingdom* (1999) 27 EHRR 611.

15 *O v United Kingdom* (1988) 10 EHRR 82. It also helped to end the immunity given to local authorities that stopped them being held accountable for negligent failure to protect them from abuse: *Z & Ors v United Kingdom* (2002) 34 EHRR 3.

16 *Malone v United Kingdom* (1991) 13 EHRR 448 (also see the 'Privacy' chapter).

17 *Chahal v United Kingdom* (1997) 23 EHRR (also see the 'Rule of Law' chapter).

18 *Darnell v United Kingdom* (1994) 18 EHRR 205.

to the rescue. It recognised the vital role of the press as public watchdog and purveyor of information on matters of public interest.[19] It emphasised that restrictions on the publication of information and opinions must be exceptional and objectively justified.[20] It ruled against the UK for using broad contempt of court laws to prevent the media from reporting on a public health tragedy[21] and to punish the public disclosure of information about a controversial prison regime involving solitary confinement.[22]

What is known as the *Ireland v United Kingdom* case showed the value of European supervision in exposing abuses that would otherwise have been condoned or covered up. It arose in the context of the longest and most violent terrorist campaign witnessed in either part of the island of Ireland. This violence found expression in part in civil disorders and in part in terrorism, that is, organised violence for political ends. Five judges were murdered in their cars. The judiciary lived and worked under constant threat of assassination, with police officers watching over them at home and in court. The 'Troubles' led to the civil rights movement, to 'Bloody Sunday', a deadly spiral of sectarian violence, and a secret war between the British security and police forces and the IRA.

Between August 1971 and December 1975, the Northern Ireland authorities used special extrajudicial powers of arrest,

---

19 *Barthold v Germany* (1985) 7 EHRR 383.
20 *Sunday Times v United Kingdom* (1979) 2 EHRR 245.
21 *Sunday Times v United Kingdom* (1979) 2 EHRR 245.
22 *Harman v United Kingdom* (1985) 7 EHRR CD146. After an admissibility decision in the applicant's favour the government wisely decided to avoid embarrassment by accepting the inevitability of defeat. It paid the applicant's legal costs and persuaded Parliament to change the law on contempt of court. (See the 'Free Speech' chapter.)

detention and internment. The Irish government brought the case against the UK, complaining of the ill treatment of men deprived of their liberty.

The European Commission of Human Rights heard evidence from 119 witnesses. It found that the Royal Ulster Constabulary had used five interrogation techniques on fourteen men, including wall-standing, hooding, subjecting detainees to continuous loud noise and depriving them of sleep, food and drink.

The English Intelligence Centre had taught the techniques as a way of extracting confessions from those suspected of terrorism. They were used in unidentified interrogation centres in Northern Ireland. They were applied in combination, with premeditation and for hours at a stretch. They caused intense physical and mental suffering, and acute psychiatric disturbances during interrogation. They aroused in their victims feelings of fear, anguish and inferiority capable of humiliating and debasing them and possibly of breaking their physical or moral resistance.

I was a member of the British legal team. The Attorney General, Sam Silkin QC, promised the Strasbourg Court that the five techniques would not in any circumstances be reintroduced as an aid to interrogation. The Strasbourg Court accepted the undertaking and agreed with the government that although the treatment was inhuman it did not amount to torture.

The Treasury Solicitor heading the government legal service was Basil Hall. He had been awarded a Military Cross for bravery during the Second World War and had been involved in the first inquiry into the 'Bloody Sunday' shootings. He had initially been sceptical about the Strasbourg system but had been impressed by the quality of the fact-finding of the European Commission of Human Rights – 'as good as a British High

Court judge'. He told me that without the Commission he doubted whether the truth would have emerged about what had happened in Northern Ireland. Basil was so impressed that, after his retirement as treasury solicitor, he served as a member of the Commission in the 1990s.[23]

Changing judicial attitudes

When I began at the Bar in 1965, the British judiciary was narrowly restrictive and executive-minded. Judges from a generation that had lived through the Second World War and its aftermath were excessively deferential to authority. There was no developed system of public law to review abuses of governmental power. Most lawyers and politicians regarded written constitutions and Bills of Rights as suitable for lesser breeds but unnecessary in our mature democracy.

During the next three decades there was a gradual but profound shift. Social attitudes changed from a climate of deference to one more critical of authority – including the attitudes of a new generation of judges. After the UK joined the European Community in 1972, judges had to interpret a system of European fundamental law and to set aside inconsistent legislation. Senior judges sitting in the Privy Council also heard appeals from Commonwealth countries and the remaining British colonies. They learned how to interpret generously

---

23 The issues raised by the *Ireland v United Kingdom* case still resonate. In December 2014, the Irish government asked the European Court to revise its judgment, after files from the UK national archive were re-examined. It is claimed that the UK withheld from the European Court what it knew about suffering deliberately inflicted on detainees and its being sanctioned at the highest levels of the UK government. The Irish government is seeking to have the treatment reclassified as torture.

guarantees of human rights modelled on the Convention and included in the new independence constitutions.

The Strasbourg Court's rulings made English judges more willing to take the Convention into account when developing the unwritten common law and reading statutes, even though Parliament had not made the Convention rights part of UK law. The way they interpreted Acts of Parliament changed from a focus on the letter of the law to considering its purpose, context and impact.

English judges decided in the mid-1970s to reform their outmoded procedures for reviewing the actions and omissions of public bodies. They later created a specialist division of the High Court to deal with applications for judicial review. Judges became adept at protecting the individual against the abuse of power. They developed principles of law that require public authorities to act lawfully, fairly, with proper authority, and in a way that does not defy logic or accepted moral standards.

Where could the judges discover those accepted 'moral standards'? By whom were they 'accepted'? Parliament had not produced a code of moral standards. The common law lacked a moral compass. Were the standards to be found in the Bible? Or in the opinions professed by the editor of their favourite newspaper? The judges were given no guidance by Parliament.

Under the UK system, an international treaty does not become part of the law of the land unless and until Parliament enacts legislation to incorporate it into domestic law. The Convention is a treaty but, even though Parliament had not made Convention rights part of our law, the new generation of judges increasingly had regard to Convention law for guidance in making their rulings – in interpreting ambiguities in the law, or in deciding moral questions about life and death.

When the Law Lords decided whether a local authority could end a mother's access to her child, they looked to the Convention right to a private and family life.[24] When they decided whether a journalist could refuse to disclose his sources to the police, they looked to the Convention right to freedom of expression.[25] They did so too when giving guidance to prevent juries from awarding excessive amounts of damages in libel cases.[26] Without any statutory mandate, they developed the common law – that is, the body of our law developed by the courts rather than by Parliament – to match the rights and freedoms protected by the Convention. They went as far as they could without trespassing on political grass.

But there were limits that confined them. Because Parliament had not made the Convention part of our law, the Law Lords felt unable to intervene to protect free speech when the Home Secretary banned Sinn Féin and the IRA from taking part in broadcasts of any kind with the aim of depriving them of the oxygen of publicity.[27] They considered that it was wrong for them to do through the back door what Parliament had failed to do through the front door. The only way that ministers could be made to comply with the Convention rights was by a new Act of Parliament – what became the Human Rights Act 1998.

---

24 *Re KD (A Minor) (Ward: Termination of Access)* [1988] 1 AC 806 (HL).
25 *Chief Constable of Leicestershire v Garavelli* [1997] EMLR 543.
26 *Rantzen v Mirror Group Newspapers* [1994] QB 670 (CA); *John v MGN Ltd* [1997] QB 586 (CA).
27 *R v Secretary of State for the Home Department, ex p. Brind* [1991] 1 AC 696 (HL). The ban had the opposite effect and exposed the government to public ridicule.

The political campaign for a Human Rights Act

For thirty long years I campaigned in favour of a Bill of Rights. Senior civil servants used sneaky tactics to fight the idea. In 1976, a Whitehall committee on which I served produced a report on the pros and cons of making the Convention part of our law. The Permanent Secretary at the Home Office tried to persuade me that the report should not be published. When he failed, Whitehall mandarins briefed the Cabinet to oppose publication. When the Cabinet rejected that advice, the Home Office craftily printed only a few hundred copies[28] and it was hardly noticed by anyone.

A year later, in Northern Ireland, officials linked with the Home Office shelved a report by the Standing Advisory Commission on Human Rights that advocated bringing the Convention into UK law.[29] I had contributed to the report as special adviser to the Committee. In 1984, another senior civil servant at the Home Office tried to stop me from being appointed chair of an Anglo-American conference on a Bill of Rights because I was biased in favour. When he failed to persuade the conference director to remove me, he insisted that Enoch Powell MP should be invited to take part. Powell enlivened the proceedings by explaining that a black person did not become British merely by being born in Britain. He also suggested that I was guilty of treason, for bringing cases in Strasbourg against the Crown.[30]

---

28 *Legislation on Human Rights with Particular Reference to the European Convention* (London: HMSO, June 1976).

29 *The Protection of Human Rights by Law in Northern Ireland*, Cmnd 7009, November 1977.

30 The sustained campaign by top Home Office officials to prevent the Convention from becoming part of our law reminded me of Herman Melville's *Moby Dick* and Captain Ahab's obsessive pursuit of the whale.

The 1980s were an ice age for constitutional reform, though Margaret Thatcher was radical in other ways. It was not until the 1990s that the tide began to turn in favour of bringing the Convention rights home. NGOs and the Institute of Public Policy Research published proposals in favour of incorporation. Members of both Houses of Parliament introduced Private Members' Bills to incorporate the Convention, and I introduced a couple of my own in the House of Lords. Two former Lord Chancellors, two former Home Secretaries, the Master of the Rolls, the Lord Chief Justice of England and Wales, leading Law Lords, the Bar Council and the Law Society came out in favour.

Before New Labour won power in 1997, Labour and the Liberal Democrats cooperated with one another in devising a programme of constitutional reform. Robin Cook and Robert Maclennan negotiated a crucial agreement bringing together key elements of constitutional reform.[31] It included making the European Convention part of UK law and setting up a parliamentary Joint Committee on Human Rights to monitor compliance with human rights.

An ingenious compromise

The Human Rights Act subtly reconciles respect for parliamentary supremacy with the need for effective remedies for violations of the Convention rights.[32] The Act does not empower the courts to

---

31 Robin Cook was a Labour Party MP, later promoted to foreign secretary in Blair's New Labour government. Robert Maclennan was an MP, President of the Liberal Democrats (and now a Life Peer). In April 2005, they published *Looking Back, Looking Forward: The Cook–Maclennan Agreement, Eight Years on* (London: New Politics Network, 2005).

32 The Act was modelled on the second of my Human Rights Bills and heavily influenced by New Zealand's Bill of Rights. Sir Kenneth Keith,

disregard Acts of Parliament that conflict with the Convention.[33] That would have made its passage through the Commons unlikely. Instead, it requires the courts to read and give effect to statutes in a way that is compatible with the Convention rights. Where that is impossible, it enables the courts to make a declaration of incompatibility. It is left to politicians to decide whether to take remedial action or leave it to the claimant to go to Strasbourg. In this way, the Act respects parliamentary sovereignty, but it is anchored in the Convention and the right of recourse to Strasbourg if the national system fails to deal with a case properly.

Our courts are in a weaker position in dealing with human rights issues than the courts of many other European and Commonwealth countries. Those courts have the power to strike down law that is unconstitutional. Ours can only declare that a given statute is incompatible with a Convention right. On the other hand, the political branches of government in the UK share responsibility with the courts in giving effect to the Convention rights. That is a great advantage.

The Act requires a minister in charge of a draft law to make a statement as to whether the Bill is compatible with the Convention before it is debated in Parliament. This might appear technical and boring but it is of real practical value. The

---

former President of New Zealand's Law Commission, and Justice of its Supreme Court, had worked with Sir Geoffrey Palmer on a Bill of Rights that was weakened during its passage. He helped me to fashion my Bill.

33 When it came to the devolution of power to Northern Ireland, Scotland and Wales, the courts were empowered to set aside incompatible legislation enacted by their legislatures. In that way the Convention provides a core of rights across the UK under our partially written British constitution. So the devolved governments must give effect to the Convention rights via the devolution legislation as well as the Human Rights Act.

statement alerts ministers and parliamentarians to the human rights implications of what they are doing. It ensures that any attempt to authorise a violation of Convention rights is properly debated.

The parliamentary Joint Committee on Human Rights was set up after the Act came into force. It looks at every government Bill and decides whether it agrees with the Minister's view that it passes muster under the Convention. It takes evidence from ministers and civil society and reports to Parliament so as to inform members of both Houses, including ministers, about the human rights implications of pending legislation. It monitors whether the UK is complying with judgments of the Strasbourg Court, and with the various international human rights treaties by which the UK is bound. It undertakes inquiries on issues affecting human rights in the UK, such as domestic violence, trafficking, children's rights and the rights of people with disabilities. It is well staffed and resourced.

When the UK joined Europe in 1972, British judges received no special training about the immense legal implications for the British system of parliamentary government and law. But after the Human Rights Act was enacted, the government waited for two years (until October 2000) to bring it into force. This allowed time to train the judiciary and the civil service about the impact of the Act. Nothing like it had ever happened before. As a result our judges were well prepared, as were the legal profession and the civil service.

Teething problems

Whenever a court or tribunal determines a question that engages a Convention right, the Human Rights Act says it must 'take into account' Convention case law. In 2004, Tom Bingham, the senior Law Lord, explained that the British courts have a duty 'to keep pace with the Strasbourg jurisprudence as it evolves over time: no more, but certainly no less'.[34] His words 'no more, but certainly no less' were repeated again and again but they created the impression that British courts must follow all decisions of the Strasbourg Court strictly and go no further. The Conservatives complained in their 2015 General Election pledge that 'problematic Strasbourg jurisprudence is often being applied in UK law'.[35] In fact, the requirement does not mean that Strasbourg judgments have to be followed slavishly as binding precedents if our courts think them wrong in principle. 'Take into account' does not mean 'bound by'.

British judges have matured in their understanding of the Human Rights Act and have become more self-confident. They have made it clear that they are not strictly bound by the Strasbourg Court's judgments.[36] They have sometimes departed from Strasbourg decisions. As a result, the European Court has thought again and changed its mind. For example, the Strasbourg Court held that it was incompatible with the right to fair trial to convict a man of sexual assault using a dead victim's witness statement.[37] The Supreme Court declined to follow this decision because the Strasbourg Court had disregarded other protections given to criminal defendants within our trial processes. As a result of our Supreme Court explaining its reasoning, the European Court modified its approach.

---

34 *R (Ullah) v Special Adjudicator* [2004] UKHL 26 §20.

35 *Protecting Human Rights in the UK: The Conservatives' Proposals for Changing Britain's Human Rights Laws,* October 2014, p. 4.

36 *R (on the application of Haney & Ors) v Secretary of State for Justice; R (on the application of Robinson) v Governor of HMP Whatton and Secretary of State for Justice* [2014] UKSC 66.

37 *Al-Khawaja v United Kingdom* (2011) 54 EHRR 23.

This dialogue between our courts and Strasbourg is important in both directions. The Convention and its case law need to be woven into the fabric of the British political and legal system, maintaining the integrity of British laws and public confidence in the way the system works. The Human Rights Act makes that possible. It encourages European law to be approached *through* UK law, rather than *around* it. In the absence of a written constitution, we need our courts to articulate our constitutional principles in their judgments.

UK involvement with European Convention law has brought great benefits to Europe as well. Because of the way the Human Rights Act works, our courts give the Convention case law higher priority than in countries such as France or Germany whose written constitutions are paramount. The standards of advocacy of British advocates, schooled in the common law tradition, are high. Even though only a tiny minority of four[38] of Europe's forty-seven states have legal systems based on the common law, we should take pride in having had a significant influence on the thinking and practice of the Strasbourg Court.

Threats from within

We rely upon the Human Rights Act together with the common law to protect us against the misuse of power. The British system is a subtle set of checks and balances. It works well for judges, lawyers and civil society, and for the devolved institutions. But it is fragile and can easily be weakened or destroyed because it is not protected as supreme constitutional law.

Because the Human Rights Act uses the Convention rights as a substitute for homegrown constitutional rights, it arouses the

---

38 The other three are Cyprus, Ireland and Malta.

hostility of Euro-sceptics. Our system has come under increasing onslaught, not from 'activist' judges but from political opportunists supported by right-wing newspapers that have made 'human rights' dirty words.

Critics of the Strasbourg Court complain of its 'activism'. They say that the Court's rulings go much further than is needed to protect human rights. In particular, they do not like the method by which the Court interprets the rights by current standards, rather than the views that prevailed when the Convention was drafted sixty years ago. They call it 'mission creep' and complain that the Court has interpreted the Convention far more broadly than its founders ever envisaged – and far beyond its proper limits.[39] There are a few judgments that they target as examples of 'activism'.

One arose in Sidney Golder's case.[40] Golder was a convicted prisoner serving his sentence on the Isle of Wight. In 1969, there was a serious disturbance in which a prison officer was hurt. The officer accused Golder of swinging vicious blows at him. Golder denied having done so and wanted to bring a claim for libel against the officer – but he was refused permission to consult a solicitor. He complained to Strasbourg that the refusal of permission impeded his right of access to the courts in breach of the Convention right to a fair trial. The puzzle for the Court was that the Convention did not specifically refer to a right of access to the courts but only to a fair, public and expeditious judicial procedure.

The Court pointed out that if the Convention were interpreted literally as applying only to proceedings already before a

---

39 *Protecting Human Rights in the UK: The Conservatives' Proposals for Changing Britain's Human Rights Laws*, October 2014, p. 3.
40 *Golder v United Kingdom* (1975) 1 EHRR 524.

court, a state could do away with its courts without breaching the Convention. It is hard to understand how the Court's judgment could fairly be cited as an example of undue judicial activism or overreach. The right to a fair hearing by an independent court would be meaningless if one had no right of access to the court. A literal interpretation of the English text of Article 6 would have had that perverse result.

Anthony Tyrer's case is also cited by critics as evidence that Strasbourg has gone beyond its mandate.[41] Tyrer was a British citizen living on the Isle of Man. In 1972, he pleaded guilty in the juvenile court to assault causing bodily harm to another pupil at his school. He was sentenced to three strokes of the birch. It was carried out in the presence of his father and a doctor. He was told to take down his trousers and underpants and made to bend over a table. Two policemen held him down while a third administered the punishment, pieces of the birch breaking at the first stroke.

In Britain judicial corporal punishment was abolished in 1948. The UK government considered it a degrading punishment in breach of violation of Article 3 of the Convention, but the Isle of Man government thought otherwise and defended its case to the Strasbourg Court unsuccessfully. The Court accepted that the treatment might have been normal at the time the Convention was drafted. But it ruled that the Convention is a living instrument to be interpreted in the light of present-day conditions. It found that Tyrer was treated as an object in the power of the authorities and that the institutionalised violence had harmed his dignity and physical integrity.[42]

---

41 *Tyrer v United Kingdom* (1978) 2 EHRR 1.
42 The indignity of having the punishment administered on his bare buttocks was an aggravating factor. The British judge, Sir Gerald

Those who accuse the Court of undue activism attack its interpretation of the Convention as a 'living instrument'. They argue that it should be read and given effect only in accordance with the values and conditions that obtained when the Convention was drafted and came into force. That is similar to the 'original intent' approach of Justice Scalia as a member of the American Supreme Court. He insisted that the American Constitution must be read strictly and literally in accordance with the original intent of the eighteenth-century gentlemen who devised it.

It is not the approach of the courts of other common law countries or of our own courts. They interpret legislation in accordance with contemporary values and conditions to avoid statutes becoming ossified relics of a bygone age. As long ago as 1930, the Judicial Committee of the Privy Council had to decide whether women were eligible under the British North America Act to become members of the Canadian Senate even though the reference to persons in the Act referred only to men.[43] The Lord Chancellor, Viscount Sankey, ruled that the Act was 'a living tree capable of growth and expansion within its natural limits'. The reference to 'persons' included women. Presumably today's critics would regard that as undue 'activism'.

The Privy Council has explained[44] that laws giving effect to

---

Fitzmaurice, dissented. He did not regard corporal punishment as degrading for juvenile offenders and admitted that his view might be coloured by the fact that he had been brought up and educated under a system in which the corporal punishment of schoolboys was regarded as the normal sanction. But significantly he did not criticise the Court for undue activism or overreach.

43 *Edwards v Attorney General of Canada* [1930] AC 124 (PC).
44 *Ministry of Home Affairs v Fisher* [1980] AC 319 (PC), *per* Lord Wilberforce.

basic freedoms call for a generous interpretation – avoiding what has been called 'the austerity of tabulated legalism'. That approach has been commended again and again by British courts. It is also Strasbourg's approach. Conservative critics would like Strasbourg and our courts to be narrowly literal. They would like the tree of justice to be petrified dead wood.[45]

Another criticism levelled at the Court is that its rulings encroach on the province of legislators, not judges. Judges are not elected and do not have a mandate to make the law. According to this view Strasbourg undermines the sovereignty of Parliament. In reality the Strasbourg Court is careful to respect the principle of subsidiarity and to leave it to the state to choose an appropriate means of giving effect to its judgments.

The UK system is alone in Europe and most of the common law world in placing Acts of Parliament beyond the reach of our courts. If Parliament enacts a racist law, there is nothing our courts can do except to make a declaration of incompatibility, leaving the alleged victim to go to Strasbourg. If the right to complain to the Strasbourg Court were removed, an executive-controlled Parliament would have absolute power.

The opponents of the Convention system give few examples of what they regard as 'judicial legislation' by activist judges.

---

45 That blinkered approach is not confined to today's English critics. The nomination of Thurgood Marshall as the first black Justice of the American Supreme Court was repeatedly obstructed by Southern Democrats on the Senate Judiciary Committee in the late 1960s, ostensibly for Marshall's support of the view that the Constitution had to be interpreted as a living instrument protecting the rights of defendants in criminal cases. Will Haygood, *Showdown: Thurgood Marshall and the Supreme Court Nomination that Changed America* (New York: Alfred A Knopf, 2015).

Their arguments are based on ideology rather than fact. The case that has aroused widespread political anger concerns prisoner voting. English law long banned all convicted prisoners from voting in parliamentary and local elections while in custody. John Hirst, a convicted murderer, challenged the ban as incompatible with Article 3 of Protocol No. 1 to the Convention, which protects 'the free expression of the opinion of the people in the choice of legislature'. He lost in the English courts but won in Strasbourg.[46]

The Strasbourg Court found that the ban on convicted prisoners was arbitrary and disproportionate. It is an automatic blanket ban treating all convicted prisoners alike, whether heinous murderers or petty shoplifters, regardless of their particular circumstances. The blanket ban is, in the Court's words, 'a blunt instrument. It strips of their Convention right to vote a significant category of persons and it does so in a way that is indiscriminate'.

The Court did not conclude that all convicted prisoners should be entitled to vote. It recognised that the 'margin of appreciation' – that is, the amount of discretion allowed to the state – is wide, and that it is primarily for the state concerned to choose the means to comply with the Court's judgment. There are many different ways of organising and running electoral systems in Europe.[47] However, any departure from the principle

---

46 *Hirst v United Kingdom (No. 2)* (2005) 42 EHRR 849. See also *Greens and M.T. v United Kingdom* [2010] ECHR 1826, and *Firth & Ors v United Kingdom* [2014] ECHR 874.

47 At least 18 European states, including Denmark, Cyprus, Finland, Ireland, Spain, Sweden and Switzerland, have no form of electoral ban for imprisoned offenders. In other countries, electoral disqualification depends on the crime committed or the length of the sentence. In some countries prisoners are only allowed to vote at certain elections. In

of universal suffrage risks undermining the democratic validity of the elected legislature. The right to vote is no longer the privilege it was seen to be in the time it was denied to women. The presumption in a democratic state should be in favour of inclusion.

Without any fuss, the governments of Cyprus and Ireland changed their rules to give prisoners a postal vote. Yet in Britain, Hirst's victory aroused fury among opponents of the Court, on the left and right of British politics. Instead of introducing a measure to comply with the judgment, Jack Straw candidly admits that, as Labour Lord Chancellor and Justice Secretary in government, he spent three years ensuring that the government took no decision in response to it.[48] He says he 'kicked the issue into touch, first with one inconclusive public consultation, then with a second'. After he lost office, Straw went to Strasbourg with David Davis, the former Shadow Home Secretary, to discuss their concerns with the President of the Court. David Cameron told the Commons that giving any prisoners the right to vote made him feel 'physically sick'.

The coalition government published a draft Bill on the eligibility of prisoners to vote. A parliamentary Joint Committee examined it and published a report in December 2013. It recommended that the government bring forward legislation to permit only prisoners serving sentences of twelve months or less to vote in UK parliamentary, local and European

---

France, certain crimes are identified which carry automatic forfeiture of political rights. Germany's ban extends only to prisoners whose crimes target the integrity of the state or the democratic order, such as terrorists. A. Horne and I. White, *Prisoners' Voting Rights*, House of Commons Library Standard Note SN/PC/01764, 11 February 2015.

48 Jack Straw, *Last Man Standing: Memoirs of a Political Survivor* (London: Macmillan, 2012), pp. 538–39.

elections. The government did not give effect to that modest recommendation.

In violation of international law, successive governments have failed to introduce a Bill to comply with the Strasbourg Court's judgments. That has gravely undermined the UK's good reputation as a state that respects the rule of law. It has set a terrible example to other states that do not respect human rights. In September 2015, the junior Minister of Justice, Dominic Raab MP, went to the Committee of Ministers of the Council of Europe to defend the government's refusal to give effect to the judgment. He came under strong attack from many governments across Europe, but the Russian Federation indicated that it might follow the UK's example, and in December 2015 passed a law allowing the Russian Constitution to trump the Convention.

Why human rights matter now

In comparison to his predecessor, Chris Grayling, Michael Gove is a welcome improvement as Justice Secretary. He promised Parliament that he would not withdraw from the oversight of the Convention system, nor weaken human rights protection. He even promised to legislate for an additional right to trial by jury. But his assurances are at best uncertain because of his attachment to parliamentary sovereignty and his refusal to abide by the final judgment of the Strasbourg Court on prisoner voting.

Human rights NGOs warn that any attempt to replace the Human Rights Act with a British restatement of civil and political rights and liberties is fraught with danger. They fear that a British Bill of Rights might be used as a way to deprive victims of the right to seek redress from Strasbourg. Their fears are not fanciful – especially given Britain's uncertain future in or outside the European Union and the way ministers play cat and mouse with the public. Our relationship with the Convention and our good reputation are harmed by the prevailing climate of hostility to European institutions.

Our elected politicians are unlikely to consent to any encroachment on parliamentary sovereignty that goes further than the compromise contained in the Human Rights Act. Without a new entrenched constitutional settlement, however, any British Bill of Rights, shorn of the protection of the Convention and the Court, would be much weaker than the Human Rights Act. That is why we must fight any attempt to damage the umbilical cord connecting us to Strasbourg.

The first priority is to prevent any reduction of the existing protection of human rights in this country. Any proposal for a homegrown British Bill of Rights must give a convincing answer to this question: would it weaken or strengthen existing protection?

When the coalition government was formed in 2010, the future of human rights was a major issue dividing Conservatives from Liberal Democrats. As a compromise they set up a Commission of political opposites to investigate the possible creation of a UK Bill of Rights that incorporates the Convention. I served on the Commission. We consulted the public about whether the UK should introduce a Bill of Rights. The overwhelming response favoured protecting the Human Rights Act from being weakened. But is it enough only to defend the status quo, especially when there is a lack of public confidence in the way we are governed? Is the present situation stable and enduring?

It was politically expedient for the Blair government to use the Convention as a substitute for a homegrown Bill of Rights. To avoid a prolonged debate about the contents of a British Bill of Rights, the Human Rights Act simply copied the Convention rights word for word, without changing their description or adding further rights. Instead of asking whether our *constitutional* rights have been infringed, the Act asks whether our *Convention* rights have been infringed. That is not the way it works in the rest of Europe and the common law world. For them the central question is whether there has been a breach of their constitutions. The Human Rights Act poses a different question – whether there has been a breach of a European treaty. Instead of bringing rights home, the Act has an alienating effect, especially among Euro-sceptics.

There is also a problem with a lack of equal protection of fundamental rights across the UK. The devolution scheme is 'asymmetric', devolving different powers in different ways to the Celtic nations of the UK. Apart from the Convention, there is no overarching constitutional framework that governs the whole of the realm. We do not have a federal system that protects core rights everywhere. That creates tricky problems.

For example, the right to freedom of speech is a fundamental right that is protected in the federal systems of Australia, Canada, Germany, India and the United States as a constitutional right. That means that lawmakers and courts of those countries are subject to the federal constitution, regardless of state or province.

In 2013, after careful scrutiny and public debate, Parliament enacted the Defamation Act to strike a better balance between free speech and reputation.[49] It applies to England and Wales and can only apply to Northern Ireland and Scotland with the consent of the devolved institutions.

---

49 See the 'Free Speech' chapter.

They did not consent and that frustrates the aim of the Act. A newspaper or broadcaster publishing across the UK may now risk a libel suit in Northern Ireland or Scotland for a statement that would be thrown out by English courts. Freedom of expression transcends political boundaries and frontiers. It is essential that there are common standards of human rights protection across the UK.

We need to replace the devolution scheme with a federal system that avoids problems like this. The rest of the common law world is governed under written constitutions. But the botched attempts at constitutional reform by recent governments do not provide hope that our political leaders will rise to the challenge.

Any move towards a British Bill of Rights could be made only after wide public consultation across the nation as a whole – and in the context of a wider constitutional debate. There is no room for complacency. The threat to our rights and to the Union will continue until we achieve an enduring new constitutional settlement. That is not likely to happen during the lifetime of David Cameron's government.

E.M. Forster's warning about the threats we face is as relevant today as it was in June 1935, when he spoke at the International Congress of Writers in Paris. His subject was 'Liberty in England'. He said this:

> Our danger from Fascism – unless a war starts when anything may happen – is negligible. We are menaced by something much more insidious – by what I might call 'Fabio-Fascism', by the dictator spirit working quietly away behind the façade of constitutional forms, passing a little law . . . here, endorsing a departmental tyranny there, emphasising the national need of secrecy everywhere, and whispering and cooing the so-called

'news' every evening over the wireless until opposition is tamed and gulled. Fabio-Fascism is what I am afraid of, for it is the traditional method by which liberty has been attacked in England.[50]

---

50 E.M. Forster, *Abinger Harvest* (London: Edward Arnold & Co, 1953), p. 64.

2

EQUALITY

*'The conquest of the earth, which mostly means the taking it away
from those who have a different complexion or slightly flatter noses
than ourselves, is not a pretty thing when you look into it too much.'*
Joseph Conrad, *Heart of Darkness* (1902)

*'The principle of Unripe Time is that people should not do at the
present moment what they think is right at that moment, because the
moment at which they think it right has not yet arrived.'*
F.M. Cornford, *Microcosmographica Academica: Being a Guide
for the Young Academic Politician* (1908)

The meaning of equality

Belief in the equality of all human beings is at the heart of liberal
thought. We all claim to believe in equality as a universal right
of humankind. Yet everywhere there is gross inequality.
Prejudice and discrimination are deep-rooted in the human
condition. Like other animals, we identify with what we regard
as our own kind, through our families and friends, our customs,

languages and beliefs. We tend to exclude or reject those to whom we feel we do not belong. As the pigs controlling government in George Orwell's *Animal Farm* cynically proclaimed, 'All animals are equal, but some animals are more equal than others.'

The challenge is to find ways to reconcile our prejudices with the noble idea of equality. The German philosopher Immanuel Kant wrote famously, 'Out of the crooked timber of humanity no straight thing was ever made.' That is true but we have to do the best we can to combat prejudice and discrimination.

Law has an important role to play but it is not a panacea. It has to be given practical reality by public authorities and private bodies exercising powers of a public nature, as well as by individual men and women. Judges interpret and apply equality law but they cannot make economic and fiscal policy. They can decide whether a policy is discriminatory or in breach of human rights because those are legal issues within their proper constitutional province. But usually it is the elected political branches of government that have to tackle problems of social and economic disadvantage and priorities of public spending, like when to introduce shared parental leave, or how to encourage candidates from minority ethnic backgrounds to apply to university, or how much public money to allocate to the Equality and Human Rights Commission.

One key principle of the idea of equality is that although human beings are different in innumerable respects, our common humanity requires that we all are treated equally on merit. That means that for every difference in treatment, there must be a good and relevant reason. It is relevant that a worker seeking employment should have the skills required for the job, or that someone wishing to buy a house should be able to pay the purchase price, or that a customer in a restaurant should behave in an orderly fashion. But it is not relevant whether the employee, homebuyer or customer is black or white, male or female, gay or straight, old or young. Race, colour, age and sexuality are human characteristics, but they tell us nothing about an individual's intrinsic qualities. A sixty year-old may be fitter than a forty year-old and many women are stronger than some men.

So the principle of equality means that it is wrong to act on the basis of stereotyped assumptions about group characteristics – for example, that Roma or Jews or migrants are dishonest, or that women are the physically weaker sex. Even if it could be shown that such assumptions were true of the group as a whole, they would not be true of every member of the group. The average man lives a shorter life than the average woman, but not every woman lives longer than every man. So it would be wrong to allow men to retire earlier just because they are men, just as it would be wrong to offer women cheaper car insurance because they are safer drivers on average.

The idea of equality involves more than the eradication of crude and overt forms of discrimination. A rule or practice may hit more at women or black people than men or white people without intention to harm them. It may not be *directly* discriminatory on the basis of sex to pay part-time workers a lower hourly rate than full-time workers but it is *indirectly* discriminatory to do so. If most part-time workers are women, the policy has an adverse effect. Such a policy can be excused only where an employer can prove it is objectively justified by the needs of the business – for example, the higher costs of training two part-time workers rather than one full-time worker.

Chief Justice Burger, giving the decision of the American Supreme Court, used Aesop's fable of the Fox and the Stork to explain the principle of indirect discrimination.[1] The Fox invited his friend the Stork to dinner and served her with soup in a shallow dish. The Fox could lap it up but the Stork could only wet the end of her long bill. The Stork invited the Fox to dine with her. In revenge, she served food in a long-necked jar with a narrow mouth into which the Fox could not insert his snout. Equality requires the Fox and the Stork to be able to feed from vessels each can use. To provide only what the Stork or the Fox could use would violate Aristotle's maxim: 'treat like cases alike; unlike cases differently'.[2]

To enable a disadvantaged minority to overcome past discrimination, the concept of equality may require positive measures to create a level playing field. Known in the USA as affirmative action, positive discrimination involves implementing measures so that disadvantaged groups enjoy full equality now, rather than waiting on the never-never land of the undefined future.

The law permits political parties to draw up all-women shortlists to contest parliamentary seats, even though this puts male candidates at a disadvantage. It is a way of making Parliament more representative of women and men. But this is a tricky area. Ethnic and religious minorities are also under-represented in Parliament. There are many more Muslims than Jews in Britain, but it would be invidious and divisive to impose racial and religious quotas to reduce the number of Jews or increase the number of Muslims in Parliament or elsewhere. Jews were victims of quotas imposed by the Nazis and would strongly resent being classified in that way.

---

1 *Griggs v Duke Power Co.* 401 US 424 (1971).
2 H.L.A. Hart, 'Principles of Justice', in *The Concept of Law* (Oxford: Clarendon Law Series, 2nd ed., 1998), pp. 157–67.

To advance equality, employers and service providers need to monitor the effects of their policies and practices. To know whether a particular group is disadvantaged or under-represented, we need evidence, usually in the form of statistics. Some European countries forbid the collection of data about race, remembering how it was abused by the Nazis to find and persecute Jews. To require people to disclose their ethnicity or gender reassignment or sexual orientation also raises problems of privacy. That can be addressed by collecting data anonymously. Without such statistics, employers and service providers cannot appreciate the extent of discrimination nor determine how to stop it.

There are now legal tools across Europe to combat discrimination on the grounds of ethnicity, religion and belief, sexuality, disability, age and pregnancy. They raise problems of definition, like what a religion is and what kinds of belief should be protected.[3] There are problems of fairly balancing conflicts of interest between different protected groups – the young versus the elderly in the competition for jobs or the effect of rising house prices, married couples versus single parents over tax breaks, and so on.

The competing interests of young and old must also be balanced. A fixed retirement age ensures that new blood refreshes the judiciary and that more women can join the bench. But for most jobs a fixed retirement age is unnecessary and unfair. Age is not a reliable indicator of experience or capacity to work. To make people retire prematurely is wasteful if they are still capable of doing the job. And who should decide how the

---

3 R (Hodkin) v Registrar General of Births, Deaths and Marriages [2013] UK SC 77. The UK Supreme Court decided that Scientology was a religion. The author was counsel for the Scientologists.

balance should be struck generally or in particular cases – judges or Parliament or ministers or employers or trade unions or individual workers?

Reconciling equality and religious freedom is particularly difficult. In a plural democratic society, cultural differences should be accorded equality of respect unless they are abusive or oppressive. What to one group is praiseworthy to another group may seem anti-social; for example, wearing a niqab from head to toe.

Deep-rooted division is true within as well as between religions. Within Christianity, Catholics and Protestants in Scotland and Northern Ireland divide themselves into separate antagonistic communities. British Sikhs disagree about whether mixed-faith marriages are permissible in Sikh temples.[4] Many followers of traditional religions seek to deny recognition to new religions or belief systems they describe as 'cults'.

Unlike France or the USA, the UK does not make a complete separation between Church and state. Church of England schools and Jewish schools receive public funding. Muslim schools should be given equal treatment. When pupils in faith schools are taught in ways that offend the secular agenda, ministers intervene and insist that 'British values' be pursued to combat extremism. But how is that to be done while respecting religious freedom? And what do we mean by 'British values'? If

---

4 Mixed-faith weddings have been disrupted by protesters. The Sikh Council says that the Sikh wedding ceremony should be reserved only for Sikhs but others say Sikhism teaches equality and acceptance and that mixed-faith marriage ceremonies should be permitted. Gurvinder Gill, 'Sikh council plea to halt mixed-faith wedding protests', *BBC News*, 24 August 2015.

they are the values of freedom of speech and the rule of law, are they compatible with demands by some British Muslims to recognise Sharia law?

Religious beliefs are often at odds with other concepts of equality. A devout Christian couple run a bed and breakfast business in their home. They regard homosexual love as morally wrong and refuse to accommodate a gay couple. The Equality Act makes no exception for religious belief in such circumstances. The same is true of the registrar who refuses for conscientious religious reasons to conduct a civil partnership or same-sex marriage even though that is a public duty imposed by Parliament. Some traditional followers of the three Abrahamic religions – Judaism, Christianity and Islam – feel undervalued and even persecuted when their objections to gay marriage are rejected. These difficult questions become toxic when religion is used as a political weapon. Equality and religious freedom then become divisive and dangerous.

Failing to achieve diversity in the workplace costs money because the brightest and best are barred from the top jobs. Yet correcting unlawful past discrimination is costly and causes resentment. Employers are allowed to exclude a person with a disability from joining their workforce if they can show that it would be too expensive to make the adjustments needed for a disabled employee – extensive modifications to office buildings, for example, to overcome access problems for wheelchair users. That cost arises because of past discrimination – the building was designed for the majority of people who use steps, without catering for a minority with different needs. Should we support a defence of reasonable adjustment more widely or would that weaken the effectiveness of the principle of equality?

What about the clash between the pursuit of equality and the protection of free speech? Feminists campaign to prevent the publication of sexist advertising or pictures of semi-naked women and girls. Racist and homophobic hate speech is deplored as an assault on human dignity likely to stir up hatred. Finding the balance that allows space for free expression is a headache for lawmakers and judges.

There are no right answers to some of these questions, but it is important to identify the relevant questions and to think about how they should be addressed.

Becoming involved

I first became involved in pursuit of *racial* justice. I am Jewish. My parents were ever grateful to the UK for giving their own parents a safe haven from the Tsarist pogroms. They retained a strong sense of their Jewish identity, but, like many British Jews of their generation, they were shy about admitting their identity because of English anti-Semitism.

Some of our European relatives were murdered during the Holocaust. The images from the death camps that I saw in newsreels at the cinema when I was nine years old will haunt me always. The dead and the living dead, barrow loads of bones and limbs, mountains of corpses, bewildered staring eyes and gaping mouths were all that remained of their humanity.

In 1947, when I was eleven, I became a pupil at the City of London School – the only public school in London that had no quota restricting the number of Jews allowed entry. It was the Liberal Prime Minister Herbert Asquith's school and its teachers were proud of its liberal tradition. Several had been prisoners of war in Germany, but I never heard them express anti-German hostility. Many Jewish pupils were Orthodox and contemptuous of those, like me, who ate non-Kosher food and played sports during the Jewish Sabbath.

The only anti-Semitism I encountered personally happened during National Service, in 1956 when my regiment was waiting to join the Suez invasion. I was the only Jewish officer. The regiment had been in Libya for many years and the regular officers were equally hostile to Arabs and other Semites. They advised me to change my identity disk to 'C of E' to reduce the risk of Egyptian torture if I were captured. I said that I would take the risk because I did not want to wear a false label. This offended my superior officer, who told me not to come to a dance in the officers' mess because he was against miscegenation. I was upset that I was apparently good enough to die for my country but not good enough to dance with the maids of Kent. I stayed away.

I arrived at Cambridge University in 1957. Prime Minister Harold Macmillan had told an audience that they had 'never had it so good'. Political self-satisfaction and complacency were widespread. Cambridge University was deeply conservative and many of its students were there because of class rather than ability. There were few women and few non-white undergraduates. A black fellow student in my college was asked his complexion in a form he had to complete. He wrote 'fresh'.

In an article in *The Spectator*, the journalist Bernard Levin exposed anti-Semitism among members of the University Appointments Board, the university's careers service. Levin had been leaked their jottings about students competing for graduate scholarships. They included phrases like 'short and Jewish with wet palms' and 'Jewish but of the refined kind'. With friends Leon Brittan and Bill Wedderburn I campaigned to remove the offending members from the Board. But most students refused to sign our petition because they did not find the remarks offensive. Our protest failed and two of the culprits were promoted to more senior academic posts.

The politics of immigration was ever entangled with the politics of race. Commonwealth migrants were settling in Britain in increasing numbers. Oswald Mosley's fascist Union Movement and White Defence League called for Britain to be kept white. In the summer of 1958, they held rallies virtually every night. Mobs of several hundred people attacked West Indian homes in what they brutally termed 'nigger hunts'. Riots broke out in Notting Hill.

In March 1960, during my final year as an undergraduate, police fired on the crowd in the South African township of Sharpeville protesting against apartheid. They killed sixty-seven peaceful protestors. I sought permission from the Fellows of my college to raise funds for the survivors and their families by putting a collection box in the entrance to the Trinity College chapel. The Fellows refused permission because they regarded the cause as 'too political'. I was glad to leave conservative Cambridge for the New World.

Into the Brave New World

I was awarded a Harkness Commonwealth Fellowship for two years of graduate study at Harvard Law School. Women had been admitted for the first time only a decade before and there was no longer a Jewish quota. Many of my fellow graduate students came from parts of the world that were soon to be free of British rule. I shared their anti-imperial values. We looked forward to the end of apartheid in South Africa, a system we hoped would soon be blown away by the winds of change. I was inspired by the progressive decisions of Chief Justice Warren's Supreme Court. The country was littered with billboards with the message 'Impeach Earl Warren' – a comment on the landmark ruling in *Brown v Board of Education*,[5] which ended racial segregation in state schools.

I learned about the benefits and burdens of a federal constitution and Bill of Rights; about slavery; the civil war; and the long campaign to persuade the American Supreme Court to end racial segregation in state schools. But I did not learn much about the reality of America's race problems or the civil rights struggles. The US Constitution's guarantee of equal protection was discussed mainly in dry terms about the extent of police powers regulating commerce between the states, not about the equality of men and women before the law. Some professors were internationally minded but there was little interest in civil rights abroad.

The race problems of the northern cities were pernicious and worsening. The growth of black ghettoes created an informal system of segregation. A black underclass was deprived of decent housing, healthcare, education and employment. Police brutality, crime and corruption were endemic. Prisons were filled to bursting point with black men.

I travelled with an Indian friend to an international law conference in Washington DC. On the way she was refused service at a bus stop in Delaware until after all the white customers had been served. In Washington DC, I could not find a hotel willing to give me a room when she was with me.

I returned to the UK reluctantly in 1962 to read for the Bar. England was asleep to its growing social problems. Discrimination was blatant and overt. Landlords were advertising vacancies with 'sorry no coloureds' and 'no blacks, no dogs, no Irish'. Pubs excluded black people. Golf clubs

---

5 *Brown v Board of Education* 347 US 483 (1954).

excluded Jews. Public schools operated quotas limiting the number of Jewish students. There were few if any black or Asian members of the police service. Police harassment of ethnic minorities was widespread. There were no black Members of Parliament.

1962 was also the year that the National Socialist Movement held its first rally in Trafalgar Square. Its leader, Colin Jordan, declared that:

> Hitler was right . . . our real enemies, the people we should have fought, were not Hitler and the National Socialists of Germany but world Jewry and its associates in this country.

Employers and trade unions colluded in race and sex discrimination in the workplace. The craft unions protected their white members. The professions were no better. Women did segregated 'women's work' and were paid less than men. They were barred from joining some leading barristers' chambers or becoming partners in law firms. Black lawyers worked in so-called 'black ghetto chambers' and many Jews worked in Jewish chambers, given work by Jewish solicitors.

During my pupillage, I witnessed a trial involving the Auschwitz doctor, Wladislaw Dering. He brought a libel case against Leon Uris and the publishers of Uris's book, *Exodus*. It alleged that Dering had performed seventeen thousand 'experiments' on prisoners at Auschwitz, using surgery without anaesthetics.

The trial brought home the horrors of the Holocaust with devastating clarity. Leon Uris and his publisher called witnesses to demonstrate the truth of the book's allegations. Victim after victim gave evidence about the barbarous atrocities to which they had been subjected as guinea pigs – the men castrated, the women having their ovaries removed. The book exaggerated the number of operations for which Dering was responsible and was therefore technically libellous. But the jury showed its contempt for him by awarding him half a penny in damages – the smallest coin in the realm.

When I had completed my pupillage the head of chambers refused to let me join his chambers. Again I was told I was 'too political' and too close to Whitehall, Westminster and Fleet Street to be a proper barrister. He was quite right!

The long hot summer of 1964

Amnesty International was then a tiny embryonic NGO led by its two founders, Sean MacBride and Peter Benenson. They asked me to go to the American South to report on racial injustice. White and black people lived in wholly separate communities. Black people could not vote. Those who stepped out of line were lynched. Slavery had been abolished but there was still a system of servitude, discrimination, oppression, racial violence and lynching.

It became known as 'the long hot summer' of 1964 and it was certainly hot in every sense. Jackson, Mississippi was the headquarters of the campaign to register black voters. A few weeks before, activists had challenged racial segregation on buses in what became known as the Freedom Rides. They were met with mob violence, police brutality and imprisonment. After investigating the burning down of a church designated for voter registration efforts, three civil rights workers – Andrew Goodman, James Chaney and Michael Schwerner – were lynched. The Ku Klux Klan burned twenty black churches that summer. Undeterred, civil rights workers pressed on registering black people to vote in elections and ran education projects in all-black schools. Lawyers from the North defended them from oppression by police and judges.

I interviewed segregationists and met a spokesman for the 'White Citizens' Council' who showed me charts comparing white and black people's skulls to illustrate the biological inferiority of 'nigrahs'. To avoid being detected consorting with the civil rights workers, I walked rather than taking taxis. I rang my friends Cliff and Virginia Durr in Alabama every night to say I was safe.

I travelled across the Mississippi Delta with a civil rights attorney. We interviewed a terrified sharecropper about his experience of race discrimination. His knees knocked so violently that his entire tin hut shook. In the small town of Rolling Fork we tried to get bail for civil rights workers. They had been arrested and locked up overnight for distributing leaflets without a permit. The next morning segregationists surrounded the courthouse. FBI agents did nothing to help us. We got away safely. Three weeks later my companion narrowly escaped being shot.

The courage of the civil rights movement led to political and legal reforms in the end. But they happened only after the Freedom Rides; the sit-ins; the bombings of churches and Sunday schools; the murder of those who stepped out of line; the march of hundreds of thousands of peaceful demonstrators on Washington; and JFK's assassination in Dallas. After so much violence, sacrifice and publicity, President Lyndon Johnson was able to muster enough political support to achieve the Civil Rights Act in 1964, the Voting Rights Act in 1965 and Thurgood Marshall's appointment to the American Supreme Court in 1967.

Campaigning at home

While I was in the American South my chambers wrote to tell me they had changed their mind about giving me a tenancy. In 1965, I began practising commercial law by day and campaigning for racial equality by night. Dr Martin Luther King had declared during a visit to London that the UK needed a civil rights movement. I was at the founding meeting of what became CARD – the Campaign Against Racial Discrimination. We campaigned for a UK anti-discrimination law modelled on US and Canadian examples.

CARD was a febrile coalition of Marxists, Maoists, Trotskyites, Soviet Communists, as well as Labour and Liberal party activists. It was chaired by David Pitt, a Labour Party stalwart GP from Grenada, who struggled to hold us together. We gathered evidence of race inequality and lobbied for change. I wrote fake job applications under the pseudonyms Smith and Singh. My alter egos were equally well qualified on paper – yet invariably Smith was offered a job interview, while Singh was not. We were thrown out of pubs in West London when we went with our black colleagues.

Labour won the 1964 General Election with a slim majority. In the face of public hostility to immigration, Harold Wilson's government promised to reduce the number of non-white workers allowed to settle in Britain.[6] At the same time the government tried to tackle race discrimination. The ailing Home Secretary, Sir Frank Soskice QC, published a Bill to make it a crime to discriminate on racial grounds or to stir up

---

6 *Immigration from the Commonwealth*, Government White Paper, Cmnd 2739 (London: HMSO, August 1965).

racial hatred. It was mistake to make racial discrimination a crime, because it would difficult to prove and not give a remedy to the victim. We managed to persuade him to make racial discrimination a civil wrong. But the Race Relations Act 1965 was narrow in scope, lacking in enforcement and satisfied no one. It did not tackle discrimination in education, housing or employment – just 'places of public resort' like hotels and restaurants.

In December 1965, Roy Jenkins took over from Soskice. He was a liberal reformer and an admirer of Jack and Robert Kennedy. I met him and pressed for a wider, more effective race discrimination law. He readily agreed but there was scant support for change within the government, the Labour Party or the trade unions.

Preparing the ground required political guile. Jenkins made speeches explaining that integration should not mean that immigrants had to lose their own national characteristics and culture. He said that we did not need a 'melting pot', turning everybody out in a common mould as one of a series of carbon copies of someone's misplaced vision of the stereotyped Englishman. Integration was not assimilation but 'equal opportunity, accompanied by cultural diversity in an atmosphere of mutual tolerance'.[7] His definition of multiculturalism would later be misunderstood to justify turning a blind eye to oppression within the new communities of migrants and their children.

Jenkins cleared the path for a new law. But in August 1967, the pound was devalued and he was moved to the Treasury, swapping jobs with Jim Callaghan. We reformers at CARD who

---

7 Speech made on 23 May 1966 on 'Racial Equality in Britain', in *Roy Jenkins, Essays and Speeches* (London: Collins, 1967), p. 26.

had been so hopeful were suddenly faced with a very different Home Secretary.[8]

Callaghan was a pragmatic realist but no liberal. When the politics of immigration once again became entangled with the politics of race, Callaghan followed rather than led public attitudes. That led to what became known as the East African Asians case.

In the early 1960s, during the independence negotiations of Uganda, Kenya and Tanzania, the British government had given British Asian citizens in those countries the option to remain British citizens with British passports. That entitled them to enter and settle in the UK. Many British Asians realised that the new governments of East Africa might strip them of their right to live there, so instead of opting for local African citizenship, they chose to keep their British citizenship.

The newly independent East African governments introduced racist policies of 'Africanisation'. They gave preference to their citizens in trade and employment and required British Asians to leave. They came to Britain in increasing numbers as British citizens with full British passports.

Two Conservative MPs, Duncan Sandys and Enoch Powell, campaigned to remove their right to settle in Britain. They pandered to public prejudice about non-white immigration. Callaghan gave in. A senior member of the government, Richard

---

8 Worse still, in December 1967, CARD was taken over by its Trotskyite/ Maoist elements, and I resigned with several colleagues. It ceased to be an effective lobby. In 1968, the publicist and writer Jim Rose and I founded the Runnymede Trust in response to CARD's decline. It is an independent think tank countering racist propaganda and advising on issues of public policy.

Crossman, recorded his impressions of the Cabinet meeting chaired by the Home Secretary:

> Jim [Callaghan] arrived with the air of a man whose mind was made up. He wasn't going to tolerate this bloody liberalism. He was going to put a stop to this nonsense [of Commonwealth immigration] as the public was demanding and as the Party was demanding. He would do it come what may and anybody who opposed him was a sentimental jackass . . . Mainly because I'm an MP for a constituency in the Midlands, where racialism is a powerful force, I was on the side of Jim.[9]

Callaghan rushed an emergency Bill through all its parliamentary stages in just three days and nights. British citizens who had not been born in the UK, or whose parents or grandparents had not been born here, were stripped of their right to enter the country. On its face the Bill was not racially motivated. But its intention was racist and so was its effect. By surrendering to the demands of extremists, it lent respectability to the idea that it was the presence of non-white people in Britain that caused social unrest.

Some two hundred thousand British Asians lost their right to enter and live in their country of citizenship. They were divided from members of their families in the UK, detained for weeks or months in prison if they sought to enter without Home Office permission; or shuttled here and there, across Europe, Africa and Asia, desperately seeking a new world. Some were stranded in Europe en route for the UK, others in India. Nominally they remained citizens of the UK and

---

9 Richard Crossman, *The Crossman Diaries*, vol. 2 (London: Hamish Hamilton and Jonathan Cape, 1976), pp. 678–79.

Colonies in fact, if not in law – but they became citizens without status.

Ministers had misused their majority in Parliament to abridge the basic rights of a group of fellow British citizens because of their colour and ethnic origins. In the absence of a written constitution protecting the rights of citizens, the Westminster Parliament was all-powerful. British courts could not declare the enactment of this obnoxious measure beyond the powers of Parliament.[10] It was a classic example of what J.S. Mill termed 'the tyranny of the majority'.

Callaghan's Race Relations Act 1968

In April 1968, a few weeks after persuading Parliament to pass his racist Commonwealth Immigrants Act, Jim Callaghan introduced a new Race Relations Bill. Pandering to racial prejudice by excluding the East African Asians did not succeed in taking race out of politics. Enoch Powell made a notorious speech foreseeing 'the River Tiber foaming with much blood'. He claimed that the Bill showed that immigrant communities could:

---

10 The only remedy open to these dispossessed victims was to complain to the European Commission of Human Rights that the UK had violated their Convention rights. I acted as their co-counsel. The Commission concluded that the applicants had been subjected to degrading treatment. To single out a group for differential treatment on racial grounds was a special affront to human dignity. *East African Asians v United Kingdom* (1973) 3 EHRR 76. The decision was a heavy blow to the UK's reputation. Roy Jenkins decided not to challenge the Commission's decision in the Strasbourg Court but to increase the rate at which they could settle in the UK.

Agitate and campaign against their fellow citizens, and . . . over-awe and dominate the rest with the legal weapons which the ignorant and the ill-informed have provided.

It was his view that the UK:

Must be mad, literally mad, as a nation to be permitting the annual inflow of some fifty thousand dependents, who are for the most part the material of the future growth of the immigrant descended population. It is like watching a nation busily engaged in heaping up its own funeral pyre . . .

That tragic and intractable phenomenon which we watch with horror on the other side of the Atlantic but which there is inter-woven with the history and existence of the States itself, is coming upon us here by our own volition and our own neglect. Indeed, it has all but come. In numerical terms, it will be of American proportions long before the end of the century. Only resolute and urgent action will avert it even now.

Heath sacked Powell from his Shadow Cabinet the day after that speech – but polling showed three-quarters of the British public agreed with it. Were he alive today Powell would no doubt claim to have been like the legendary Cassandra, an accurate prophet of doom.

The new Race Relations Act 1968 was broad in scope, outlaw-ing discrimination in employment, housing and public services. But it was weak in enforcement. It made the Race Relations Board (a statutory body set up by the 1965 Act) the sole avenue of legal redress for discrimination's victims. They had to go through futile conciliation procedures before taking their grievances to the Board. The process was costly, time-consuming and ineffectual.

Yet even a toothless law was too much for the legal estab-
lishment. In February 1969, Viscount Radcliffe, a former Law
Lord, gave a public lecture echoing Enoch Powell. Radcliffe
declared that Britain was host to a 'large alien wedge' that
carried with their colour 'a flag of strangeness and all that
strangeness implies'.[11] He claimed that race discrimination was
not condemned in society, so should not be condemned by
the law.

The Law Lords interpreted the Race Relations Act narrowly.
It prohibited discrimination based on national origins as well as
colour and race. But when Irish and Indian nationals living in
the UK were barred from council housing waiting lists, the Law
Lords decided that 'national origins' did not include nationali-
ty.[12] The Law Lords also declined to assist a British Asian refused
membership of his local Conservative Association because of
his colour. They claimed that the Association was a private body
and therefore outside the scope of an Act applying to public
services. It was preposterous to consider as 'private' a political
club organised to influence the fate of the nation.

Another regrettable decision involved Mr Sherrington, a
black member of a 'working men's club'.[13] His club was part of a
union that enabled members from similar clubs to enjoy one
another's facilities. Yet when he went with some friends to the
Dockers' Labour Club and ordered drinks, he was refused
service because of the club's colour bar. The Court of Appeal

---

11 Lord Radcliffe, 'Immigration and Settlement: some general consid-
erations', *Race,* vol. 11, No. 1 (1969), pp. 35–51.
12 *Ealing London Borough Council v Race Relations Board* [1972] AC 342
(HL).
13 *Race Relations Board v Dockers' Labour Club and Institute Limited*
[1974] QB 503 (CA).

decided that the refusal contravened the Race Relations Act –
but the Law Lords overturned the decision.[14]

Equality for women

Unequal pay for women was another ancient and persistent
problem of deep-rooted discrimination. In 1968, Ford
Dagenham sewing machinists went on strike. They made car
seat covers, and their action eventually halted all car production.
The strike lasted three weeks. Inspired by their example,
women trade unionists founded a National Campaign for
Women's Rights. In May 1969, there was an equal pay demonstration in Trafalgar Square.

In response Parliament passed Barbara Castle's Equal Pay
Act in 1970. It was another mouse of a law, the product of a
deal done with employers and trade unions – both sides male-
dominated. It dealt only with crude forms of sex discrimination. It covered equal pay for the same work, but not for different work of equal value. Its coming into force was delayed for
five years.

I gave evidence for the Labour Party to a Lords Committee
examining a Private Member's Bill on sex discrimination.[15]

---

14 *Dockers' Labour Club and Institute Limited v Race Relations Board* [1976]
AC 285 (HL). The Court of Appeal had interpreted the Lords' decision in the
Charter case as permitting the Dockers' Labour Club to enforce a colour bar so
as to refuse membership to a man because he was black. But they decided that
the club could not enforce a colour bar against an associate of the union. The
Law Lords, however, treated the case as analogous to that of a private household
involving domestic or social intercourse and the choice of one's friends. I did
not foresee that I would be able to advise the government to reverse these decisions in the Race Relations Act 1976.

15 The Bill was introduced in 1972 by Baroness Nancy Seear with strong

Baroness Edith Summerskill was a committee member and a doughty champion of women's rights. She said that my proposals had no hope of becoming reality.

In February 1974, Harold Wilson became Prime Minister but without a majority in the Commons. Labour's election manifesto promised to bring in legislation against sex and race discrimination. Wilson appointed Roy Jenkins as Home Secretary for a second time. Before the Election, I had written a policy paper, with my wife Katya, setting out our proposals for a Sex Discrimination Bill. We sent it to Jenkins. He invited us to lunch and explained that he lacked confidence that his junior Minister and civil servants would produce effective legislation. He asked Katya to become his special adviser but she was heavily pregnant. So he asked me instead, wryly joking that he would have two for the price of one.

I soon discovered why Jenkins needed support. Senior Home Office officials had advised the previous Conservative government to adopt a narrow approach to sex discrimination legislation. They no doubt hoped that the Wilson government would not last long. They were especially opposed to giving strategic law enforcement powers to the proposed new agency – the Equal Opportunities Commission – and wanted the Bill to include a series of unnecessary exceptions.

From the outset I was given a frosty reception by the Home Office team. It led to several weeks of trench warfare. When I discovered that Home Office officials had deviously concealed from me the views of Department of Employment ministers and civil servants that supported mine, I told Jenkins I could not

---

support from the Labour and Liberal benches but was opposed by the Conservative government. The Bill died through lack of parliamentary time.

work under such conditions. He sent me home to write the White Paper on *Equality for Women*.[16]

The White Paper promised direct access to tribunals and courts and publicly funded assistance for sex discrimination claims. It envisaged that the Equal Opportunities Commission would be responsible for investigating systemic discrimination and bringing strategic legal proceedings to enforce the law.[17] I had wished to strengthen the Equal Pay Act 1970 as part of a broader reform package. Unfortunately, the government considered the Act an unalterable bargain between employers and unions.

The Sex Discrimination Act became law in December 1975, the same time that the Equal Pay Act came into force. It gave birth to the Equal Opportunities Commission. The Race Relations Act followed a year later, with a companion Commission for Racial Equality. Administrative agencies of this kind were commonplace in North America but novel in the UK. Ministers had difficulty in recruiting qualified people as commissioners and the civil service declined to send high flyers to administer them. When the Commissions

---

16 *Equality for Women*, Cmnd 5724, Home Office (1974).

17 I made an embarrassing mistake in the White Paper by writing that the concept of discrimination was concerned with the proof of the motive or intention of the discriminator. It was only when I went to the USA with Jenkins in December 1974 and was reminded of US equality law that I realised my mistake. Luckily, we persuaded ministers to include the concept of indirect discrimination in the Bill, but it was drafted in such narrow and technical language, appropriate to income tax but not civil rights legislation, that it took many years of costly UK and European litigation to get it right: *Bilka-Kaufhaus GmbH v Weber von Hartz*, 170/84 [1984] ECR 1607; *DH & Ors v Czech Republic* (2008) 47 EHRR 3, §184. It is not always well understood even now.

were challenged in judicial review proceedings, the courts found them wanting. That sapped confidence and discouraged the use of their important legal powers to tackle systemic discrimination.

The incoming tide from Europe

Help to strengthen our legislation came from an unanticipated quarter. In April 1976, the European Court of Justice in Luxembourg gave a momentous decision. Gabrielle Defrenne, a cabin attendant for a Belgian airline, had been paid less than her male counterpart in the same job. To the surprise of the European Commission and governments, the Luxembourg Court ruled that the European principle of equal pay had direct effect. That meant that it could be directly relied upon in national courts and tribunals without the need for national legislation to implement it.[18]

To English lawyers, schooled in the doctrine of parliamentary sovereignty, the decision was mind-boggling. It meant that European Community law trumped national law – and the Sex Discrimination and Equal Pay Acts had to be construed in light of it.

Armed with this new weapon, the Equal Opportunities Commission supported sex discrimination test cases before the European Court. The idea was to use Community law to overcome defects in our equality legislation. It was a risky strategy because the losing party usually pays the winner's costs; and the Commission's entire budget could have been exhausted by a single costly defeat.

I acted for the Equal Opportunities Commission in some of

---

18 Case 43/75, *Defrenne v Sabena* [1976] ECR 455.

the early test cases, before judges who had difficulty in interpreting the new legislation. Wendy Smith was a manager. She was paid less than the man she had replaced, even though she did the same work as he had. Read literally, the Equal Pay Act allowed her to compare her work and pay only with a man working at the same time, not with a predecessor. In the Court of Appeal only Lord Denning was willing to read the legislation sensibly, in light of the European principle of equal pay for equal work.[19] So the case was sent to the European Court of Justice. It ruled in Wendy Smith's favour and parliamentary sovereignty had to yield.[20]

Mrs Shields brought a case of sex discrimination against a South London betting shop. Her employer claimed her lesser pay was necessary because she did not have 'maleness', a quality that deterred troublemakers from the shop. I explained to Lord Denning that some men (like me) are more cowardly and less physically strong than their wives. Denning gave me a pitying look. Probably imagining my petite wife Katya to be built like an Olympic discus thrower, he ruled that:

> The only difference between the two jobs is on the ground of sex. He may have been a small nervous man, who could not say 'boo to a goose'. She may have been as fierce and formidable as a battle axe.[21]

---

19 *Macarthys Ltd v Smith* [1979] ICR 785 (CA).
20 Case 129/79, *Macarthys Ltd v Smith* [1980] ICR 672. When the case came back to the Court of Appeal, it interpreted the legislation to comply with European law, effectively rewriting the language of the Equal Pay Act: *Macarthys Ltd v Smith* [1981] QB 180 (CA).
21 *Shields v E. Coomes (Holdings) Limited* [1978] 1 WLR 1408 (CA).

The 'Troubles' in Northern Ireland

Across the Irish Sea, a different form of discrimination festered. For fifty years, between 1921 and 1972, the Official Unionist Party had ruled the region. The first Northern Ireland Prime Minister, James Craig, described his government as a 'Protestant government for Protestant people'. It abolished proportional representation for elections, gerrymandered election seats and discriminated against Catholics in the allocation of jobs and housing. Instead of responding, for fifty years successive governments in Whitehall and the Westminster Parliament turned a blind eye to this injustice.

In the 1960s, young Catholics, influenced by the civil rights movement in the USA, had led civil rights protests that focused worldwide attention. The Unionists refused to budge. Towards the end of the decade, the IRA began a campaign of violence and Protestant loyalists responded in kind. There were horrifying scenes of bomb and bullet, murder and maiming, bereavement and mutilation. People lived in a situation unparalleled elsewhere in Western Europe since the Second World War. The situation was described euphemistically as the 'Troubles'. It was akin to a state of civil war.

The security situation escalated and the Heath government began to intern IRA suspects without trial. Serious mistakes in policing and military action culminated in what became known as 'Bloody Sunday' in January 1972. At a protest march, British soldiers fired over one hundred rounds into fleeing crowds. They shot twenty-six unarmed civilians, killing thirteen people on the spot.

The Northern Ireland Parliament was abolished in 1973. Heath's government imposed direct rule that continued when Harold Wilson won the General Election in February 1974.

Among the avalanche of reforms that followed was the Fair Employment (Northern Ireland) Act in 1976. It outlawed discrimination on the grounds of religion and belief and set up a Fair Employment Agency to promote equality in the workplace. The Act was strengthened in 1989, after a powerful campaign in the USA to withhold investment unless Margaret Thatcher's government brought in the necessary changes.[22] The Northern Ireland legislation was progressive but designed completely separately from Parliament's measures to tackle sex and race discrimination. Our governors did not permit it to be copied in Britain, so equality legislation became divided by the Irish Sea.

Disability

In the 1980s, the anti-discrimination agenda expanded to include disability rights. People with disabilities had been viewed historically with pity, ridicule and hatred – as objects of charity, not active participants in society. They were systematically excluded from communal life. Public and private sectors designed facilities and services to suit the majority and failed to consider those with different needs. Visually impaired people were blocked from access to education by a national curriculum constructed for the majority who learn by sight, rather than the minority who read through Braille. The old attitude saw the

---

22 The MacBride Principles are a corporate code of conduct for US companies doing business in Northern Ireland. They were launched in 1984 and became the Congressional standard for US aid to Northern Ireland – threatening to end investment in Northern Ireland unless the law was reformed. It was strengthened in 1989 by Margaret Thatcher's government, which introduced measures to give effect to the MacBride Principles. The Fair Employment and Treatment (Northern Ireland) Order 1998 then further reformed equality law.

medical condition as the disabling factor, rather than minority exclusion. Any assistance to people with disabilities was viewed as charity – optional, laudable, kind. The government arranged services *for* disabled people – but it opposed the use of law to combat disability discrimination.

By 1994, Canada, Australia and the USA had all enacted disability discrimination legislation. But the UK government's position was that education and persuasion would do the trick. Ministers argued that enforcement agencies were too costly and that legislation might destroy employers' goodwill towards disabled people.[23]

In 1994, Dr Roger Berry, a Labour MP, introduced a Private Member's Bill that had wide parliamentary support.[24] Alf Morris MP was its architect. The Bill was supported by a coalition of organisations of and for disabled people, all united under the name 'Rights Now!' Campaigners sent two hundred and fifty thousand postcards to MPs urging their attendance to debate the Bill. Just before the debate, a two-thousand-strong crowd lobbied Parliament.[25]

John Major's government blocked the Bill's progress by tabling eighty different wrecking amendments.[26] It ran the debate out of time but generated publicity for campaigners.

---

23 *Employment and Training for People With Disabilities,* Department of Employment Consultative Document, 1990, §5.14–5.15.

24 Civil Rights (Disabled Persons) Bill 1994.

25 The vast majority were people with disabilities and Westminster's inaccessibility to them strengthened the case for change. See Roger Berry MP's 'A Case Study in Parliamentary Influence', *Journal of Legislative Studies*, vol. 2, issue 3, 1996, pp. 135–44.

26 The MPs were all Conservative backbenchers – but the government officially denied responsibility for the amendments: HC Deb 4 July 1994, vol. 246, cols. 3–4.

Belatedly the government gave way and resolved to introduce a disability rights law. It was enacted in 1995 and in 1999 New Labour created a Disability Rights Commission to enforce it.

There were now three equality commissions – the Equal Opportunities Commission, the Commission for Racial Equality and the Disability Rights Commission, as well as the Fair Employment Agency in Northern Ireland.

Sexual orientation discrimination

Sexual orientation discrimination joined the equality agenda in the 1980s. In 1967, homosexual sex had been decriminalised in England and Wales. Scotland had followed suit thirteen years later. In 1978, the UK government had published a proposal to bring the law in Northern Ireland into step with the rest of the UK. But resistance to decriminalisation was deep-rooted. None of the twelve Northern Ireland Members of Parliament openly supported reform. Several opposed it. Roman Catholic bishops argued that changing the law would lead to further decline in moral standards and to 'a climate of moral laxity that would endanger and put undesirable pressures on those most vulnerable – namely the young'. The Protestant Church cautioned that relaxing the law might be interpreted as 'an implicit licence if not approval for such practices'.[27] So the government abandoned the idea.

A year later, Jeffrey Dudgeon complained to the Strasbourg Court. Police officers had searched his home in a drugs raid and found evidence that led them to suspect that he might be 'guilty' of 'gross indecency between adult males'. He was asked

---

27 *Dudgeon v United Kingdom* (1981) 4 EHRR 149, §25.

to go to the police station and questioned for four and a half hours about his 'homosexual activities'. Although the authorities decided that it was not in the public interest to press charges against him, the very existence of the criminal offences caused him fear and suffering – and left him vulnerable to harassment and blackmail. The Strasbourg Court decided the risk of prosecution had a chilling effect on the enjoyment of his right to respect for a private life. The offence was repealed a year later, in 1982.

Despite the ruling, homosexuality remained a valid ground for discharging members of the armed forces long into the 1990s. Armed forces policy guidelines stated that homosexual relationships could 'cause offence, polarise relationships, induce ill-discipline and as a consequence, damage morale and unit effectiveness'. Commanding officers were instructed to launch a formal investigation – with assistance 'where necessary' from the service police – against any serviceman or woman suspected of being gay. Once 'outed', they were automatically dismissed, never to serve again.

Where those under investigation 'confessed' their sexuality, officers proceeded to 'verify' the 'admission'. Jeanette Smith had been a nurse in the RAF since 1989. In 1994, a woman telephoned the Air Force alleging that Ms Smith was a lesbian. Ms Smith was questioned by the service police and told them that she was gay. She was asked intimate questions about the details of her sexual life, names of previous partners, her HIV status and other details. She was even asked whether she and her partner had a sexual relationship with their sixteen-year-old foster daughter.[28]

---

28 The government accepted during the proceedings that it was indefensible to have posed this question.

Graeme Grady, a sergeant who had been a member of the RAF since 1980, was asked about his marital difficulties, his sleeping habits and what 'type' of sex he had. Investigators searched his accommodation and rifled through his diary for evidence of 'homosexual contacts'.

Jeanette Smith and Graeme Grady challenged the legality of their dismissal from the RAF. So did Lieutenant Commander Duncan Lustig-Prean and weapons mechanic John Beckett, who were dismissed from the Royal Navy after long service solely because of their sexuality. An anonymous letter to Mr Lustig-Prean's commanding officer, and Mr Beckett's confiding in a service chaplain, had prompted the investigations. They were both asked intrusive and offensive questions.

In 1996, our courts accepted that there was no evidence that an individual's sexuality affected their ability to carry out their work, or had a negative effect on discipline. Each of those dismissed had exemplary records.[29] But although the courts sympathised with the victims and doubted whether the policy would long survive, they felt unable to conclude that it was so unreasonable as to be unlawful.

Three years later, the Strasbourg Court decided that neither the investigations nor their discharge on the ground of their sexuality was justified.[30] The decision was initially controversial because some argued that it would disrupt service morale. But Tony Blair's government abolished the policy a year later, rejecting the official opposition arguments against complying with the ruling.[31]

---

29 *R v Ministry of Defence, ex p. Smith & Ors* [1996] 2 WLR 305 (CA).
30 *Smith and O'Grady v United Kingdom* (1999) 29 EHRR 493.
31 The decision has come to be widely accepted in the armed forces. In

We were still far from true equality. English law gave full effect to the bond between lawfully married couples but gay couples were barred from marrying. After the death of their loved one, the surviving partner could not enjoy full rights to communal property. Unlike widows or widowers, they were not relieved of inheritance tax on the death of their partner. They could not receive next-of-kin entitlements, such as a pension. It was common that the surviving partner was forced to move out of the couple's home because the deceased's family refused to recognise their relationship.

In 2002, I introduced a Private Member's Civil Partnerships Bill to enable unmarried couples (both opposite-sex and same-sex) to enter into civil partnerships. The Bishop of Winchester described the Bill as:

> Destroying a precious ecosystem on which the security, the maturing, the well-being and the wholesomeness, not only of countless individuals but of our society, now and in the future, depends.[32]

But the government responded by introducing its own Bill. Civil partnership is as good as marriage in all but name, granting all the rights and obligations of civil marriage to any same-sex couples that registered. Tony Blair faced down opposition from Northern Irish politicians who tried to prevent it from applying to the Province. Ironically, the first civil partnership ceremony took place in Belfast.

October 2008, the outgoing head of the British Army, General Sir Richard Dannatt, told delegates at a lesbian, gay, bisexual and transgender conference that respect for others was 'not an optional extra'.
32 HL Hansard, 25 January 2002, cols. 1691–1746.

A blind eye to minority oppression

Britain's race discrimination problems used to be seen as problems of colour, that is, discrimination based on the colour of Commonwealth immigrants and their families. When almost fifty years ago, Roy Jenkins defined racial integration as involving 'equal opportunity accompanied by cultural diversity in an atmosphere of mutual tolerance' he did not mean that society should turn a blind eye to oppression within or by Britain's new communities. But that is how 'multiculturalism' came to be misunderstood by public bodies, with tragic consequences for the victims of forced 'marriage', 'honour' crimes, female genital mutilation, caste discrimination and unregistered Muslim 'marriages'.

The forcing of children and young adults to marry against their will is a pernicious social evil. Often the victims are removed from school at fifteen or younger and taken abroad where they meet a stranger and are coerced into a legal union. They suffer abuse and often rape. A few who refuse to submit risk being murdered as victims of what is grotesquely called an 'honour' crime.

Jasvinder Sanghera is one victim who has documented her story. She was born to Sikh parents who had settled in Derby. She had seven sisters, most of them older, and as she grew up she watched as they were taken out of school, one by one, to marry men they had only seen in photographs. At fifteen, her father locked her in her bedroom and refused to let her out unless she agreed to marry a man she had never met. She ran away to Newcastle. When she made contact with her family, they derided her as a prostitute for defying them, then disowned her as an outcast.

Her sister Rabina suffered horrific abuse in her 'marriage'. She committed suicide by setting herself on fire, leaving behind a four-year-old son.[33] When I went to Jasvinder's book launch in Derby in 2007 I discovered that the local authority had refused to allow the installation of a helpline in the local state schools, in deference to the elders of the Sikh community.

In 2006, the Blair government set up a Forced Marriage Unit to tackle the problem.[34] The government decided that forced marriage should not be a criminal offence because there were already adequate crimes dealing with its elements – abduction, kidnapping, rape, murder and harassment.

I believed that the civil law could offer an effective remedy. If victims and concerned friends or family members could apply for an injunction to prevent a forced marriage, the civil law could remedy the evil – and do so without needing victims to turn over members of their own family to the police to face criminal charges and possible imprisonment.

I took advice from the Southall Black Sisters (an NGO working for black and minority ethnic women), women's refuges and family law practitioners and together we crafted a Private Member's Bill so that those concerned could apply to a judge for a forced marriage order to protect a victim. The judge would then include any measures needed, like confiscation of the victim's passport so she could not be forced overseas to a ceremony with a foreign 'husband', or restrictions on the 'husband' contacting the victim. Hearings would take place in private, so orders could be made without

---

33 Jasvinder Sanghera described the violence and cruelty involved in her book, *Shame* (London: Hodder & Stoughton, 2007).
34 It runs a helpline giving advice and support to victims in some 1,500 cases a year – the tip of the iceberg. In extreme situations, it also organises the rescue of British citizens held against their will overseas.

dishonouring the victim's family (provided that they complied).

The Bill gained huge support during the debates and Prime Minister Blair did a U-turn and supported it.[35] It came into force in November 2008 and has worked well. There is a pressing need for matching legislation in Bangladesh, India and Pakistan to protect British Asian young girls and boys from being forced into 'marriage'.

Towards a single equality act

By 1997, when New Labour won power, equality law as a whole had become a sprawling mess of inconsistent legislation.[36] Each new measure added to its incoherence, inconsistency and opacity. There were three different enforcement agencies for gender, race and disability discrimination, all barred from sharing information with one another. It was impossible to keep creating new agencies as new types of discrimination emerged. The situation cried out for reform.

---

35 Hansard HL, vol. 688, part 34, cols. 1319–1367. The Bill was debated for five hours on 26 January 2007, with 34 speakers taking part, almost all supportive. The Minister in charge, Cathy Ashton, played a key role with her officials at the Ministry of Justice in turning my Bill into one fit to be enacted.

36 Bob Hepple QC, Mary Coussey and Tufyal Choudhury, *Equality: A New Framework, Report of the Independent Review of the Enforcement of UK Anti-Discrimination Legislation* (Oxford: Hart Publishing, 2000), Appendix 2. By 2000, there were no fewer than 30 Acts, 38 statutory instruments, 11 codes of practice and 12 EC directives directly relevant to discrimination. Religious and sexual orientation discrimination became unlawful under the Equality Act 2006, and age discrimination under the Employment Equality (Age) Regulations 2006.

I went with Bob Hepple, the leading equality law expert, to meet the Home Secretary, Jack Straw. We asked him to set up an independent review of the law. Straw was responsible for race relations but he refused. He said that other ministers dealing with women's rights were unlikely to agree to the idea. We pressed on anyway and secured funding for what became the Hepple report.[37] It set out a new framework for reform supported by equality agencies, judges, employers and trade unions.

Tony Blair and his government were not interested, so I introduced a Private Member's Bill based on the report's recommendations.[38] It was debated in 2003 with wide support. The Minister told the Lords optimistically that things would never be the same, but then the Government took six more years to introduce its own Bill.

In 2006, Ruth Kelly MP became Minister for Women and Equality. It was a controversial appointment because of her religious objections to homosexuality and her lack of enthusiasm for reform. The government brought in an Equality Bill that put the cart before the horse. Instead of creating a coherent legal framework, it set up a single Equality and Human Rights Commission, the EHRC. It had a woolly aspirational human rights mandate that risked blunting its cutting edge – tackling systemic patterns of discrimination.[39] I had argued in favour of

---

37 The final report was *Equality: A New Framework, Report of the Independent Review of the Enforcement of UK Anti-Discrimination Legislation*, Bob Hepple QC, Mary Coussey and Tufyal Choudhury (Oxford: Hart Publishing, 2000).
38 The Equality Bill 2003. It was drafted by parliamentary counsel Stephanie Grundy.
39 The wording of the mandate was: to 'support the development of a society in which ... there is respect for and protection of each

two separate agencies (an Equality Commission and a Human Rights Commission) but the government insisted on only one (on grounds of cost).

Another mistake was Trevor Phillips's appointment in 2006 to chair the EHRC. He had chaired the Commission for Racial Equality and opposed the creation of the EHRC, claiming it would undervalue the need to tackle race discrimination. Yet he was given the top job. The EHRC became divided and politicised – more an NGO than a public regulator and enforcement agency. Six commissioners resigned after expressing concerns about the chair's leadership and probity. They alleged that there was a conflict of interest arising from his ownership of shares in a private consultancy firm.

A parliamentary select committee on which I served prepared a critical report about Phillips's alleged misconduct.[40] He was investigated for his alleged attempts to influence the report. He was cleared of contempt of Parliament but told that his behaviour had been inappropriate and ill advised.[41] Senior and experienced equality staff had retired because they doubted that the EHRC would give priority to eliminating discrimination.[42] Instead of replacing him, Harriet

---

individual's human rights, and for the dignity and worth of all'. Section 3 Equality Act 2006.

40 Joint Committee on Human Rights, *Equality and Human Rights Commission*, 15 March 2010, Thirteenth Report of Session 2009–10, HL Paper 72/HC Paper 193.

41 House of Lords Committee for Privileges and Conduct, *Mr Trevor Phillips: Allegation of Contempt*, 5 July 2010, First Report of Session 2010–11, HL Paper 15, §14.

42 The Joint Committee on Human Rights had also expressed concerns that bringing the human rights agenda into a single commission would weaken enforcement of equality law: Joint Committee on Human Rights,

Harman reappointed Trevor Phillips, and he remained in office after Gordon Brown's government lost the 2010 General Election.

Having botched the creation of the EHRC and wasted years by failing to reform equality law, Labour at last introduced a single Equality Bill in 2009. It came at such a late stage in the parliamentary session that it was touch-and-go whether it could pass before the 2010 General Election. I led for the Liberal Democrats in the Lords. We tried to improve the Bill while avoiding unnecessary amendments that would delay its passage. It squeaked through just before the General Election.

The Equality Act 2010 was worth the fight. It harmonises the concepts of discrimination, harassment and victimisation and protects the characteristics of age, disability, gender reassignment, marriage and civil partnership, race, religion or belief, sex and sexual orientation. The Act applies to employment, housing, education and the provision of services. It requires public bodies to combat discrimination and promote equality. It permits positive action. It forbids treatment with a discriminatory effect even if it is done without hostile intent.[43]

Coalition politics

Though it is a model law, the Act was attacked when the coalition came to power. Senior Conservative ministers sought to thwart it

---

The Case for a Human Rights Commission, 3 March 2003, Sixth Report, Session 2002–03, HL Paper 67–1, HC 489–1.

43 Regrettably the Equality Act 2010 does not apply in Northern Ireland and the right to equality remains defined and protected differently across the Irish Sea.

for ideological reasons. One of Prime Minister Cameron's close advisers apparently wanted to abolish it completely. Liberal Democrat ministers blocked that foolish proposal.

The government issued a 'Red Tape Challenge' to scrap unnecessary regulation burdening business. The EHRC was an obvious target of the austerity cuts. The equality side of its work became a grin without a cat.[44] It had a large budget that was hard to justify because of the EHRC's lacklustre performance and weak financial control. The budget was radically cut and its helpline was taken away, even though it had proved a vital link with potential victims.

The coalition then persuaded Parliament to weaken the legislation in several respects,[45] all of which were unnecessary. More encouragingly, it introduced equal marriage legislation in 2013, enabling same-sex couples to marry in England, Wales and Scotland – though not in Northern Ireland, where resistance remains deep-rooted.[46] The government also introduced shared parental leave, giving working families with newborn babies the option to divide time out from work more equally between mother and father. It made the breach of a Forced Marriage

---

44 '"Well! I've often seen a cat without a grin," thought Alice; "but a grin without a cat! It's the most curious thing I ever saw in my life."'
Lewis Carroll, *Alice's Adventures in Wonderland*, Chapter 6.
45 By removing the Employment Tribunals' power under section 124(3)(b) Equality Act 2010 to make wider recommendations in discrimination cases. And by removing the questionnaire procedure under section 138 Equality Act 2010.
46 In November 2015 the Northern Ireland Assembly voted to legalise same sex marriage by a slim overall majority of 50.5%. However, the Democratic Unionist Party tabled a Petition of Concern at the outset of the debate to the effect that the proposal could only succeed if a sufficient number of both unionist and nationalist MLAs backed it. Not enough Unionists voted in favour.

Protection Order a crime and created a specific crime of forced marriage, punishable by fourteen years' imprisonment.

The coalition also oversaw the first ever joined-up strategy to tackle female genital mutilation (FGM) in the UK. FGM happens when a female, usually a young girl, has her genitals brutally mutilated to keep her sexually 'pure'. It can involve removal of the clitoris or inner labia, narrowing the vagina or otherwise damaging it by pricking, piercing, cutting, scraping or burning. FGM gives rise to wounds, infections, psychological trauma, tetanus, gangrene and even death. Some one hundred and seventy thousand victims in this country are living with the consequences of FGM. It affects an estimated sixty-five thousand girls under the age of thirteen each year.[47]

Though it had been a serious criminal offence since 1983 and thousands of women had been treated in hospital for the after effects, there was not a single prosecution for FGM until 2015. The crime was not reported to the police until 2010. Campaigners were refused access to schools to raise awareness because of a misunderstood notion of multiculturalism that feared stigmatising 'certain ethnic groups'.[48]

It took an anonymous NSPCC helpline for the first cases to be reported to prosecutors – and a damning report by the Commons Home Affairs Committee before the issue was taken up by politicians in earnest. In April 2014, the Education Secretary, Michael Gove, wrote to every school in Britain warning about its dangers. The government set up a special unit,

---

47 Home Affairs Committee, *Female Genital Mutilation: The Case for a National Action Plan*, 25 June 2014, Second Report of Session 2014–15, HC 201.
48 'The battle to eliminate FGM is long, but it's one we must win', *Guardian*, 28 June 2013.

trained public sector workers to recognise abuse and legally obliged doctors, teachers and social workers to report FGM.

For obscure political reasons, the Conservatives in the coalition were less keen to tackle another invidious form of minority oppression: caste discrimination. It is an ancient problem, imported into this country as a result of the migration and settlement of British Asians. Britain has never had a caste system but it has always had a class system – difficult for foreigners to perceive without a life-worn sense of it. Westerners have similar problems comprehending caste. We often try to fit caste discrimination into categories that we have created and to which we therefore relate: discrimination based on skin colour, apartheid, social immobility, forced labour. No one in the UK overtly condones caste discrimination but there are those who benefit from treating low-caste or no-caste people badly.

The National Institute of Economic and Social Research produced clear evidence that it was occurring – in education, employment and the provision of public goods and services. The Anti-Caste Discrimination Alliance campaigned to include caste as a protected characteristic in the Equality Act.[49]

Parliament amended the law accordingly but the coalition declined to implement it, using the worn-out argument that the problem should be tackled through education rather than law.[50] After three years of government inaction, the House of Lords tried to force the government's hand. It passed an amendment placing ministers under a legal duty to implement the change.[51]

---

49 Section 9(5)(a) Equality Act 2010.
50 Department for Culture, Media and Sport, Ministerial Written Statement, Caste, 1 March 2013.
51 Section 97 Enterprise and Regulatory Reform Act 2013.

Yet the Conservative side of the coalition flouted the will of Parliament and continued to make excuses for inaction. The EHRC concluded that urgent action was needed but that made no difference. David Cameron's government continues to refuse and the law remains uncertain.[52]

The way ahead

From the 1960s, the Westminster Parliament shed some ancient prejudices and developed anti-discrimination laws, culminating in the Equality Act in 2010. Yet across each of the protected characteristics there is still a long way to go.

Colour bars have been abolished and race discrimination is unlawful. There are prominent black and Asian judges and MPs in both Houses of Parliament. But hidden forms of discrimination are prevalent in employment, housing, education and public services. Five times more black people are imprisoned in England and Wales[53] and black people are six times more likely than white people to be stopped and searched by the police.[54] Black and minority ethnic recruitment is meagre.

Ethnic and religious minorities are scapegoated across Europe, especially Muslims, Jews and Roma. Fanatics commit

---

52 EHRC Research Report 91, *Caste in Britain: Socio-legal Review*; EHRC Research Report 92, *Caste in Britain: Experts' Seminar and Stakeholders' Workshop*.

53 Equality and Human Rights Commission, The First Triennial Review, *How Fair is Britain? Equality, Human Rights and Good Relations in 2010*, Executive Summary, p. 10.

54 Equality and Human Rights Commission, *Stop and Think: A critical review of the use of stop and search powers in England and Wales*, March 2010, p. 3.

terrorist outrages in the name of Islam. Many Muslims condemn them but are scared to do so in public. Extreme right-wing political groups exploit popular fears of a threat to their safety and way of life from uncontrolled migration. Hate crime against Muslims has hugely increased. Anti-Semitism is on the march again.[55]

The gender pay gap has narrowed but remains. Female managers in the UK earn twenty-two per cent less than their male counterparts. The difference in pay amounts to one hour and forty minutes of unpaid labour a day.[56] Women shoulder the bulk of childcare and domestic work, still work in lower-paid sectors and are still kept out of senior jobs.[57] We have shared parental leave and women make up half the workforce – but only a third of managers, directors and senior officials are women, only a quarter of boardroom executives, a third of MPs and just seven per cent of engineers. There has been some small erosion of white male dominance of the judiciary in England and Wales but progress in gender diversity is glacially slow. Only one of the twelve Supreme Court Justices is a woman. Since Baroness Hale took up the position in 2004, fourteen more justices have been appointed to our highest court – all of them men.

In countries that long ago made sex between same-sex consenting adults a serious crime, lawmakers and judges have

---

55 The Community Security Trust recorded 1,168 anti-Semitic incidents against Britain's Jewish population in 2014, more than double that in 2013. *Antisemitic Incidents Report 2014*, The Community Trust, p. 4.

56 Jennifer Rankin, 'Female bosses are working for free as gender pay gap persists', *Guardian*, 25 August 2015.

57 David Perfect, *Gender pay gaps*, Equality and Human Rights Commission, Briefing Paper 2, Spring 2011, p. 12.

recognised gay love as equal in the eyes of the law. Same-sex marriage is legal in many countries in and beyond Europe, including Britain (but not Northern Ireland). Yet over half of gay teenagers report homophobic bullying or discrimination at school.[58] The Irish Republic voted in a referendum in 2015 to permit gay marriage – but the Northern Ireland government still fails to do so.

Almost half of all children in England and Wales are born to unmarried parents. Cohabiting couples often think, wrongly, that their legal entitlements are protected by a so-called 'common law marriage'. In reality there is no such thing and when the relationship breaks down, the partner who is not the breadwinner suffers great injustice. The risk of poverty is made worse for the children of separating cohabitants. I have tried many times in Parliament to make civil partnerships available to opposite as well as same-sex couples. I failed in 2004 because other parliamentarians said that it would undermine marriage.

I tried and failed again in 2008, when I launched a Cohabitation Bill to protect unmarried couples who had lived together for two years, or had a child. It gave them limited rights to make a claim for financial support at the end of their relationship. It reached Committee stage in 2009 but the government was unwilling to support it. It died in 2010, when Labour lost the General Election. It was opposed by Conservative ministers as undermining marriage. It remains important unfinished business.

Asylum seekers are treated with distaste and suspicion on racial grounds. They reach Europe in huge numbers in the

---

58 *Boys Who Like Boys*, Report by the National AIDS Trust, 9 March 2015, p. 4.

anarchic aftermath of wars and regime changes in Africa and the Middle East. In 2014, the UK government ended its contribution to an operation that rescued thousands of North African refugees drowning in the Mediterranean as they attempted to reach Europe. Nearly four million people fled Syria in fear of persecution. It was a humanitarian crisis reminiscent of the refugees fleeing from Nazi and Soviet forces in the last months of the Second World War, but the UK treated it as a security issue.

In the summer of 2015, there was a crisis in Calais as desperate refugees repeatedly stormed the Channel Tunnel terminal in an effort to reach the UK. French and British politicians blamed each other for what they called the Calais 'jungle' and Prime Minister Cameron offensively referred to a 'swarm' of migrants. More than three hundred members of the legal community signed a call for urgent and humane action to establish safe and legal routes to the UK and Europe. Their concerns were not addressed. David Cameron is a master of public relations but has no long-term strategy other than to ensure his own survival. Europe's leaders have little sympathy for his political problems but can be fairly criticised themselves. They have failed to coordinate the sharing of responsibility for migrants and refugees across the EU.

The Equality Act is a model law, but it is as much under threat from the Cameron government as the Human Rights Act. Neither law is an ordinary law. They are as much bulwarks against the misuse of power as the written constitutions of most other democracies. They are the sinews of British democracy and by weakening them we harm ourselves.

A new generation now has the opportunity to give the ideal of equality better practical reality through public governance and the voluntary action of individual men and women. I hope that they will overcome problems that we could not solve. Complete equality is an unattainable ideal, but we must come a good deal closer if we are to remain a civilised society.

3

FREE SPEECH

'If liberty means anything at all, it means the right to tell people what they do not want to hear.'
George Orwell, Preface to *Animal Farm* (1945)

'We must be stronger at standing up for our values, and we must be more intolerant of intolerance, taking on anyone whose views condone the extremist narrative or create the conditions for it to flourish.'
David Cameron (29 June 2015)

We all cherish the right to free speech. Or rather, we cherish our *own* right to communicate freely. But what about the right of other people to free speech – those who maliciously attack our reputation, or who invade our private lives to sell newspapers? What about artists or writers whose works are condemned as 'blasphemous' or 'obscene', or who offend religious beliefs or moral values like the novelist Salman Rushdie, threatened with death for insulting the Prophet? Or *Gay News*, found guilty of blasphemy for publishing an explicit homoerotic poem about

Jesus? What about preachers of race or religious or homophobic hatred, or those who deny the Holocaust?

The 2006 Terrorism Act made 'glorifying' terrorism a crime, but did not define what 'terrorism' meant. It is sweepingly broad. We would have no qualms about applying the crime to Jihadist murderers who gunned down cartoonists to avenge the Prophet, or who used digital videos of beheading or burning hostages as a weapon of war. Yet liberals like me worried that the crime might have applied to Nelson Mandela and the ANC and their supporters in their armed struggle against apartheid in South Africa, or to the memoirs of an IRA leader. What is the difference? Is it just a question of which side you are on?

What about hate speech that falls short of stirring up violence? Should free speech trump the need to avoid racial or religious or homophobic hatred? Should race, religious, homophobic and disability hate speech be treated in the same way? Should free speech stop feminists from banning national newspapers from featuring photographs of topless models?

How do we weigh other important values that may limit free speech – such as the protection of personal privacy, the right to a good reputation, or official secrecy? Should elected officials be more open to attacks on their reputation, or their privacy, than the ordinary citizen? When journalists refuse to disclose sources vital to putting a criminal behind bars, should they be able to claim that they have acted in the public interest? When they steal or breach confidences in pursuit of an important story, should they be able to claim a public interest defence?

There is no single organising principle that enables us to resolve such dilemmas, but we have to try to do better than say that it all depends on the context and a sense of proportion.

Free speech was declared by the United Nations in 1948 to be a universal right. But that is a hope, not reality. Different countries have very different attitudes to free speech. At one end of the spectrum, the First Amendment to the United States Constitution is strong medicine, interpreted as giving free speech near-absolute protection. It requires the father of a fallen soldier to endure a hateful protest against homosexuality at his son's funeral. It allows women to be confronted by the opponents of abortion during the fraught moments before they enter clinics.[1] It permits Pastor Terry Jones to burn the Qur'an knowing that his action will lead to mass protests and unrest across the Muslim world.

At the other end of the spectrum, the rulers of China,[2] Russia and Saudi Arabia[3] suppress and punish political dissent, shut down websites and censor access to the internet. Europe is somewhere in the middle. It gives high protection to political speech and journalism but also restricts free speech in favour of other aspects of the public interest. What counts as 'proportionate' restriction leaves wide scope for different interpretations.

The digital revolution has made it easier for anyone to reach a wide audience and to campaign. Previously marginalised voices are now heard and their stories circulated. The web's anonymity provides a cloak for whistleblowers when they publish secrets.

---

1 Adam Liptak, 'The First Amendment's Limit: the Supreme Court's Plaza', *New York Times*, 14 October 2014. In *McCullen v Coakley*, 134 S. Ct. 2518 (2014), the US Supreme Court struck down a law in Massachusetts which criminalised knowingly standing on a 'public way or sidewalk' within 35 feet of an entrance or driveway to any place (other than a hospital) where abortions are performed. It was held to violate the First Amendment because it burdened 'substantially more speech than necessary' to achieve the interests of public safety, order, promoting free flow of traffic, protecting property rights and protecting a woman's freedom to seek pregnancy-related services. However, there is a federal law in place prohibiting force or threat of it to intimidate or interfere with the provision of reproductive health services.

At the same time, it creates new opportunities for abuse – for hackers, cybercriminals, blackmailers and terrorist groups seeking to diffuse their propaganda across the world. The web has enabled more intrusive invasions of our private lives by government agencies and private companies than the world has ever known. It exposes publishers to legal liability in multiple jurisdictions under diverse laws. At the same time, it is a platform for anonymous defamatory attacks to be published and republished in seconds, to audiences all over the world. Its cross-border reach undermines the effectiveness of national laws that limit, protect and enhance free speech. Yet attempts to regulate the web to protect data privacy are a regulatory minefield.

I have grappled with these dilemmas in the courts and in Parliament. They are perplexing and difficult. My bias is in favour of free expression. I have represented newspapers in many cases in which the common law fell short in protecting free speech. It was strengthened by the European Convention on Human Rights, which (mostly) strikes a fair balance between free speech and the rights of others, including the right to privacy. I will explain where I stand, what has been achieved, where we have failed, and the threats we now face.

Our culture of liberty is deep-rooted – a political and philosophical heritage we trace to thinkers such as Milton, Wilkes, Paine

---

2 Authorities in Guizhou province announced plans in December 2014 that would place university lecturers under constant CCTV monitoring to ensure the exclusion of politically sensitive subjects. Leo Lewis, 'Cameras spy on China's academics', *The Times*, 4 December 2014.

3 Raif Badawi's Free Liberals website encouraged debate on religious and political matters in Saudi Arabia. He was sentenced to ten years' imprisonment and 1,000 lashes for running the website. Ian Black, 'Global outrage at Saudi Arabia as jailed blogger receives public flogging', *Guardian*, 11 January 2015.

and J.S. Mill. But fifty years ago, free speech was not an enforceable legal right in the UK. It was a political value rather than a legal entitlement. It could be trumped by whatever Parliament of the day regarded as more important – public order, or national security, or protection against the corruption of public morals. The Lord Chamberlain had the power to decide how much nudity should be allowed on stage. The law forbidding obscene publications threatened writers and their publishers with criminal prosecution. Overbroad speech crimes haunted our common law – remnants of crimes created by the King's men in medieval times. Our judiciary failed to take a principled approach to weighing free speech against other aspects of the public interest.

The right to freedom of expression is protected in Article 10 of the European Convention on Human Rights. The Strasbourg Court's rulings in UK cases, finding breaches of Article 10, have changed UK laws for the better. It was our membership of the Convention system and its use in British cases that persuaded our judges to discover and develop the common law protection of free speech that we enjoy today.

Contempt of court

Take the old common law crime of contempt of court. It involved restricting media reporting to ensure that a case was fairly tried. In the 1960s and 1970s, the thalidomide disaster came to light. The highest court in the UK, the House of Lords, used contempt of court law to suppress important information about a drugs company, Distillers. Distillers manufactured and marketed a drug called thalidomide, given to pregnant women suffering morning sickness.

But thalidomide interfered with the development of the foetus. Many of the children of women who had taken it were born with deformities – blindness, deafness, damaged internal organs, shortened limbs, or no limbs at all.[4] More than four hundred families were affected in Britain and at least another ten thousand elsewhere in the world.

Some British families sued Distillers for negligence but negotiations over a settlement became protracted. In 1968, sixty-five families accepted an offer of compensation in return for withdrawing their lawsuits. But by 1971, several hundred families were still awaiting redress. Some children affected reached the age of twelve without compensation to manage their disabilities. They were left to endure the ordeal alone. The government and the lawyers representing the families viewed them as victims of an unforeseeable disaster rather than a tragedy that could have been prevented if the drugs company had not failed in its duty of care.

Harry Evans, the feisty editor of *The Sunday Times*, campaigned for justice. His paper accused Distillers of negligence, pointed to its huge profits and criticised its settlement offer as grotesquely out of proportion to the injuries suffered. At the time the drug was marketed, Distillers had assets of more than £4 billion at today's values and pre-tax profits of more than £500 million in today's prices. Harry Evans informed the Attorney General he would publish a piece tracing how the tragedy had occurred.

The government won an injunction to prevent him from doing so. The Attorney General said the article might prejudice a fair settlement, by putting pressure on Distillers to increase its offer. If it had that effect, publication would amount to contempt of court, a common law crime.

---

4 The campaign is described in Sir Harold Evans' autobiography *My Paper Chase: True Stories of Vanished Times* (London: Abacus, 2009), Chapter 15.

Harry Evans' memoir recalls how the scandal became the most emotionally draining of all in which he was involved at *The Sunday Times*. Enoch Powell MP was Minister of Health from 1960 to 1963, at the time when no family had received a penny in compensation. Powell rejected their pleas for assistance. He refused to set up a public inquiry on the causes of the disaster. He also refused to issue a warning to any mothers who might still stock the pills in their medicine cabinets. In his view, it would amount to a scaremongering publicity stunt.

The Sunday Times mounted an expensive legal challenge against the injunction. It was successful in the Court of Appeal[5] – but the Law Lords overruled the decision and unanimously decided that the gag order should remain. Their ruling gave scant attention to freedom of expression or the public's right to be informed. So Harry Evans took the case to Strasbourg for *The Sunday Times*. I was his barrister. He tried to acquire support from other newspapers – without success. Among the British media, dog eats dog.

By a narrow margin the Court found in favour of *The Sunday Times*, in 1979.[6] It explained that the Convention guarantees not only the freedom of the press but also the right of the public to receive information on matters of public interest and concern. The thalidomide families had a vital interest in knowing all the underlying facts. The article was moderate and balanced. By bringing information to light, it might have served as a brake on

---

5 *Attorney General v Times Newspapers* [1974] AC 273 (HL). The Court decided that the public interest in the matter outweighed the interests of the parties in a fair settlement. The law did not prevent comment on dormant litigation or settled cases; and the pressure that the article was bringing to bear was legitimate.
6 *Sunday Times v United Kingdom* (1979) 2 EHRR 245. The decision in favour of the newspaper was made by a wafer-thin majority of 13 to 11 votes.

unenlightened discussion about the drugs company's role in the tragedy, rather than inflaming it.

In the wake of that victory, Parliament enacted a new law on contempt of court, the Contempt of Court Act 1981. It removed much uncertainty in the old law and enabled those accused to defend themselves on the basis that they had acted in the public interest. The legislation would not have happened without Strasbourg's ruling.[7]

But our most senior judges – the Law Lords – continued to show a lack of sympathy for freedom of expression. One extraordinary instance arose in Harriet Harman's case.[8] Before she became a Labour MP, Harriet Harman worked as a solicitor for the National Council for Civil Liberties (now known as 'Liberty'). She acted for Williams, a prisoner, against the Home Office. Williams had been kept in solitary confinement – as part of a special regime for dealing with particularly disruptive prisoners. He challenged the legality of this treatment. Harriet Harman promised the Home Office that if it gave her access to confidential documents about the regime, she would use them only for the purposes of the case.

Journalists covered the trial. The relevant parts of these documents were read out in open court by Williams's barrister,

---

7 What the Strasbourg Court decided was of huge significance to the thalidomide families because it enabled them to obtain compensation from Distillers, which manufactured and marketed the drug on licence in the UK. But to this day Harry Evans continues to campaign for justice for the other victims across the world against Chemie-Grünenthal, the German company that originally developed thalidomide. See Harold Evans, 'Thalidomide: how men who blighted lives of thousands evaded justice', *Guardian*, 14 November 2014.

8 *R (Harman) v Secretary of State for the Home Department* [1983] 1 AC 280 (HL).

Stephen Sedley, but the judge ruled most of them inadmissible. Afterwards, Harriet Harman allowed David Leigh, a journalist working for *The Guardian*, to inspect the documents that had been read out. He published an article criticising the prison regime. He used the documents as evidence that the Home Office knew that the regime might well be unlawful.

Most people would think that the documents lost their confidentiality as soon as they were read out in open court. Most people would think that the newspaper had acted in the public interest. Yet, for allowing the journalist to see them, Harriet Harman was convicted of contempt of court and a majority of the Law Lords upheld the conviction. Lord Diplock in the leading judgment claimed bizarrely that the case was not about freedom of speech, freedom of the press, or open justice. Two of the five Law Lords dissented from the ruling – relying on the right to freedom of expression guaranteed by the Convention.

Harriet Harman complained to Strasbourg – to what was then the European Commission of Human Rights. I represented her. After a two-day hearing (those were the happy days for advocates when there was ample time for full hearings), the Commission declared her case could go forward. The government wisely accepted the inevitability of defeat. It paid Harriet Harman's legal costs and agreed to change the Rules of Civil Procedure.

Breach of confidence and official secrecy

Official secrecy was another area that gave scant attention to the importance of free speech. Margaret Thatcher's government went to extraordinary lengths to use official secrecy and breach of confidence to prevent the press from publishing extracts from Peter Wright's book *Spycatcher: The Candid Autobiography of a*

Senior Intelligence Officer.[9] Wright had been Assistant Director of MI5. He wrote his memoir from the safety of Tasmania after retiring from the service. In it, he alleged that there had been a plot by MI5 and the CIA against the Prime Minister, Harold Wilson. A Soviet defector had secretly accused Wilson of being a KGB agent. The book also alleged that MI5 had eavesdropped on Commonwealth conferences and plotted to assassinate Egypt's President Nasser during the Suez Crisis.

The government tried to ban *Spycatcher* from being read by the public wherever it could. The Attorney General won a court order preventing publication in England and Wales. But the book became popular all over the world. The government could not prevent publication in the USA, because the First Amendment to the American Bill of Rights gives near-absolute protection to freedom of speech.

But the government tried to ban the book in Australia. It dispatched the Cabinet Secretary, Sir Robert Armstrong, to defend the realm against its former spy. Sir Robert was cross-examined by a show-stealing advocate and politician, Malcolm Turnbull (who became Prime Minister of Australia in 2015). The government had claimed in a letter to the publisher that it did not have a copy of the book. Armstrong was questioned about whether the government had lied:

Q: So that letter contains a lie, does it not?
A: It contains a misleading impression in that respect.
Q: Which you knew to be misleading at the time you made it?
A: Of course.
Q: So it contains a lie?

---

9 Peter Wright, *Spycatcher: The Candid Autobiography of a Senior Intelligence Officer* (New York, Viking, 1987).

A: It is a misleading impression, it does not contain a lie, I don't think.

Q: What is the difference between a misleading impression and a lie?

A: You are as good at English as I am.

Q: I am just trying to understand.

A: A lie is a straight untruth.

Q: What is a misleading impression – a sort of bent untruth?

A: As one person said, it is perhaps being 'economical with the truth'.

The Australian court ruled that the book was no longer secret because it had been published in the USA. So the government lost the case in the glare of humiliating publicity. Armstrong faced ridicule for the phrase 'economical with the truth'. It passed into popular usage as a result of the case.[10]

That was only the beginning. English newspapers attempting to report Wright's allegations remained gagged by the Lords' ruling in spite of the Australian verdict. The government had not banned the book's import from abroad – so *The Sunday Times* and *The Observer* argued that it was too late to protect any sensitive information. The book was freely available in Scotland and North America and could be lawfully brought into this country. In any event, it was surely in the public interest that the allegations be exposed to sunlight. But the government refused to accept defeat and pursued its attempt to obtain a ban in the English courts.

The Law Lords upheld the ban, and the majority even extended it to censor reporting of the trial in Australia. Lord

---

10 Though it can be traced back to Edmund Burke's *Letters on a Regicide Peace*, published in 1796.

Bridge (in the minority) trembled indignantly when he explained the extension.

The *Daily Mirror* contemptuously published upside-down photographs of the three Law Lords in the majority with the caption 'YOU FOOLS!' British editions of *The Economist* ran a blank page with a boxed explanation that:

> In all but one country, our readers have on this page a review of *Spycatcher*, a book by an ex-MI5-man, Peter Wright. The exception is Britain, where the book, and a comment on it, have been banned. For our 420,000 readers there, this page is blank – and the law is an ass.

Garland's cartoons in the *Independent* said it all and adorn my study today. One portrayed a grotesquely braying ass holding a placard: 'Injunctions upheld – ban on reporting Australian court case'. Margaret Thatcher was Queen Titania. The caption read: 'Titania, Thou art as wise as thou art beautiful' (*A Midsummer Night's Dream*). Another cartoon showed a distraught Margaret Thatcher on her knees, vainly attempting to light matches so she could burn piles of copies of the book.

The newspapers took their case to Strasbourg. The European Court upheld the English injunctions, up to the moment when the information became publicly available. It reasoned that doing otherwise would undermine the judiciary's authority – and maintaining the judiciary's authority was needed to protect national security.[11] But the Court warned of the dangers of censorship – because 'news is a perishable commodity and to delay its publication, even for a short period, may well deprive it of all its value and interest'.

---

11 *The Observer and The Guardian v United Kingdom* (1991) 14 EHRR 153; *The Sunday Times v United Kingdom (No. 2)* (1991) 14 EHRR 229.

TITANIA: THOU ART AS WISE AS THOU ART BEAUTIFUL. (A MIDSUMMER NIGHT'S DREAM)

Undeterred, the government sought a permanent injunction in a yet further round of litigation in England. It argued that newspapers should be duty-bound to protect national security and the government's confidential information, even when the information had been leaked and was publicly available. The newspapers argued that the public have a legitimate interest in information about how their democratically elected government and its agencies behave. Government information is not the government's private property to be hidden under a cloak of secrecy – unless it has proof that it is necessary in the national interest. In any event, the information was already in the public domain, so there were no secrets left to keep.

The High Court took account of the Convention and the Strasbourg Court's judgment in the thalidomide case. It refused to grant a permanent ban on publishing excerpts from the book. The government appealed and lost – first in the Court of Appeal and then in the House of Lords. Lord Bingham said he would not 'seek to emulate the fifteenth century pope who issued a papal bull against Halley's comet'.

Peter Wright died a millionaire from the profits of his book. I argued the case sixteen times in all, in London, Hong Kong and Strasbourg as a member of what we called 'the *Spycatcher* Bar'. Twenty-one British judges were involved with a regiment of well-paid lawyers (of which I was one) as the government continued to flog a dead horse. The losers were the taxpayers, who funded the government's march of folly.

Common law libel

Libel law involves restricting falsehoods that have or might cause harm to another person's reputation. It has been used to vindicate a lie. There is a question about how far it should be available to organisations, corporations and governments. Repressive governments often use defamation law against their critics to deter and punish political dissent. In 2010, Alan Shadrake, a British author and former journalist, was arrested in Singapore on charges of criminal defamation because his book *Once a Jolly Hangman* was critical of Singapore's judicial system. It followed previous instances where Singapore's leaders had sued journalists and political opponents for defamation. Mr Shadrake was convicted of contempt of court and spent several weeks in prison.

The fate of Eric Campion in Britain in the 1970s showed the profoundly unjust working of the English common law of libel. He had distributed a leaflet criticising the local government, Bognor Regis Council, at a political meeting. It was headed 'Save Bognor Group' and underneath the headline, it read: 'HORRIFYING, DISTURBING AND ALMOST EVIL – couldn't think of a better description of Bognor's toytown Hitlerism local government myself, Mr. Editor!'

The leaflet alleged that the Council had ignored its voters' wishes and certain councillors had abused their position for financial gain. The Council sued. Mr Campion represented himself. The judge ruled he had no defence and a bad motive. He ordered him to pay the Council £2,000 in damages, as well as its lawyers' fees.[12] The Council had not suffered any actual damage – but Eric Campion was ruined.[13]

---

12 *Bognor Regis UDC v Campion* [1972] 2 QB 169.
13 The case was criticised with characteristic brilliance and brutality by J.A. Weir, 'Local Authority v Critical Ratepayer', *The Cambridge Law Journal*, 30, 1972, pp. 238–46. The article was so sarcastic that I did not use it in the *Derbyshire* case for fear of causing offence to the judges – an act of self-censorship.

The issue arose again in the 1990s, when *The Sunday Times* published critical articles about Derbyshire County Council. They alleged that the Council leader, David Bookbinder, had made improper investments. The two pieces were headlined 'Revealed: Socialist Tycoon's Deals with a Labour Chief' and 'Bizarre Deals of a Council Leader and a Media Tycoon'. The Council, as well as David Bookbinder and the businessman, sued. That was unusual. The Council was made a party so that if the case was lost the costs would be borne by the Council and ratepayers would foot the bill, not David Bookbinder. The key issue was whether the Council could do this.

A private individual can sue to protect a personal reputation. A business can sue to protect a trading reputation. But *The Sunday Times* objected to the very idea that a local authority or government body could sue to vindicate a so-called 'governing reputation'. The threat of a libel suit might quiet those with valuable criticism of the government. That would be unhealthy for democracy and have a chilling effect on the exposure of corruption and inefficiency.

Derbyshire County Council relied on the Campion case to make its argument. It won in the High Court. But *The Sunday Times* appealed successfully to the Court of Appeal by invoking the Convention right to free speech – even though the Convention had not yet been made part of our law. When the case came to the Law Lords, they overruled Campion. They held that the Council should be open to uninhibited criticism because it was democratically elected.[14] A public body such as a local authority could not sue for libel unless it could

---

14 *Derbyshire CC* v *Times Newspapers* [1993] AC 534 (HL). We also relied upon the landmark decision of the American Supreme Court in *New York Times v Sullivan* 376 US 254 (1964).

demonstrate that the person who made false attacks on its reputation had acted in bad faith, or recklessly.[15]

Derbyshire set out the position for public authorities. It left open whether *individuals* holding public office (ministers, councillors, civil servants) should be able to sue for defamation in the same way as a private citizen. The courts addressed that question when Albert Reynolds, twice Prime Minister of Ireland, sued *The Sunday Times* for libel.

As Irish Prime Minister, Albert Reynolds had appointed a Catholic Attorney General. It was alleged that the Attorney General had mishandled an attempt to extradite a serial child abuser – a Roman Catholic priest – to Northern Ireland because it would have undesirable ramifications for members of the Catholic hierarchy. When Reynolds and his Cabinet decided later to approve the Attorney General's promotion to the Presidency of the Irish High Court, the ensuing political controversy led to Reynolds's resignation and the government's downfall.

The Sunday Times alleged that Reynolds had misled the Irish Parliament and his Cabinet colleagues when he supported the promotion. It claimed that he had backed the Attorney General for the job even though he had known all along that his excuses for mishandling the extradition did not hold water. These were very serious allegations on a matter of public interest in the UK – not least because Albert Reynolds was a chief architect of the Northern Ireland peace process.

I acted again for *The Sunday Times*. We could not prove that the article was true. We argued that as long as the newspaper had stuck to the ethics of responsible journalism, its political coverage should be protected from defamation suits – even if

---

15 This is a tort known in law as 'malicious falsehood'.

what it reported later turned out to be untrue. We advanced the idea that *political* reporting should be given special protection – because of the importance of political debate to a healthy democracy.

The Law Lords thought this would push the balance too far in favour of free speech at the cost of protecting reputation. They pointed out that there are matters of public concern other than political issues, so it was not right in principle to elevate political information to a special category.

Lord Steyn asked what I thought about German constitutional law on free expression. I confessed that I hadn't a clue. 'Well, you had better find out overnight,' he replied. I did so with a sinking feeling.

German constitutional law looks to the principle of proportionality. In each individual case, it considers relevant factors and then weighs the public interest in publication against the claimant's right to a good reputation. The trouble is that it is hard to predict how a court will decide. That makes it difficult for editors to know whether it is safe to go ahead with publishing a story. They err on the side of caution – which is to say, self-censorship.

The Law Lords developed a new defence based on this German approach.[16] They suggested a list of factors to be considered, including whether the article gave an indication of both sides of the story and whether the newspaper had tried to verify its sources. But they gave no guidance about the weight attached to each of these factors.

As we feared, the press found the defence of little practical value. English libel law continued to chill free speech and to protect reputation too strongly. However, there was a silver

---

16 *Reynolds v Times Newspapers* [2001] 2 AC 127 (HL).

lining in that case. The Law Lords recognised that freedom of expression is buttressed by the Human Rights Act 1998 – and that any attempt to curtail it would be legal only if it was 'convincingly established by a compelling counter consideration'. The constitutional presumption had finally shifted in favour of free speech, rather than its exceptions.

That presumption was evident when the Law Lords considered a defamation case relating to Corporal Lee Clegg. He was a paratrooper sentenced to life imprisonment for murdering a teenager in Belfast. Many believed he was innocent of the crime. A group of his supporters called a press conference in 1995, as part of their campaign for his release. When *The Times* wrote an article about the event, the authors included in it a criticism of Corporal Clegg's solicitors. The firm sued *The Times* for libel.

The newspaper relied on the fact that it had published a fair and accurate report of what had transpired in a public meeting. Parliament had created a defence to libel in those circumstances – but it was unclear whether a 'public meeting' included a press conference. Giving strong support to free speech, the Law Lords decided that it did. The case was argued a day after the Human Rights Act had come into force. However, Lord Steyn said that even before the Act 'the principle of freedom of expression attained the status of a constitutional right'. Lord Bingham described the press as 'the eyes and ears of the public to whom they report'.[17]

It is safer to treat freedom of expression as a British constitutional common law right than to rely exclusively on the Convention case law. The prime responsibility for securing the

---

17 *McCartan Turkington Breen v Times Newspapers Ltd* [2001] 2 AC 277 (HL).

fundamental right to freedom of expression is that of the UK, not Strasbourg. The European Court does not seek to take the place of national judges, governments or legislatures and nor should it. And although the Strasbourg Court's decisions have influenced the way in which free speech has become recognised as a fundamental right, the Court's case law on free expression is uncertain and sometimes weak. It has sometimes given too much weight to reputational rights, personal privacy and to the need for 'responsible journalism'.[18] It has rightly protected political speech in the face of moral or religious objections but failed to give equivalent protection to artistic expression.[19]

Parliament to the rescue

By the early 1990s, we had come a long way since the days of the thalidomide tragedy. British judicial attitudes had changed radically. Yet there were limits to how far we could expect the courts to improve the protection of free speech by reforming the common law. Judges are not lawmakers. They are constrained by past precedents. If they clarify and modernise the law, it is through cases that happen at random. Their task is to do justice in particular circumstances, not to consult experts and the public and consider the general application of the law. Wider reforms require parliamentary intervention.

---

18 E.g. *Lindon, Otchakovsky-Laurens and July v France* (2008) 46 EHRR 761; *Von Hannover v Germany* (2005) 40 EHRR 1; *Flux v Moldova (No.6)* Application No. 22824/04 (Lodged on 10 July 2003).
19 E.g. *Otto Preminger Institut v Austria* (1994) 19 EHRR 34; *Wingrove v United Kingdom* (1997) 24 EHRR 1; *IA v Turkey* (2007) 45 EHRR 30.

We have pressed to abolish unnecessary restrictions on free speech. Parliament abolished vague speech crimes[20] – archaic offences dating back to medieval times, used by the King's men to consolidate his rule. Although outmoded and obsolescent, there was enough life in these offences to make it important to bury them.

'Defamatory libel' was the criminal offence of causing harm to the reputation of another person. It was notoriously vague and the risk of prosecution was chilling. One miscreant punished by the Court of Star Chamber was fined, whipped, had his ears cut off, his nostrils split and his cheeks branded with the initials 'F' and 'A' to denote he was a 'false accuser.' He was then sent to the workhouse, where he was sentenced to remain for the rest of his life. His crime was harming the reputation of various noblemen by accusing them of murdering the Duke of Buckingham. Other commoners were indicted and similarly sentenced for libels ranging from singing scurrilous verses about a neighbour to laughing out loud at a reading of a defamatory verse.[21]

'Seditious libel' originally involved inciting disorder by expressing contempt towards a political authority. It was based on the assumption that rulers had the right to command the obedience of their subjects. Prosecutions could be brought even when the offender's words caused no actual harm to the authority's reputation – and even when their words were true. Over time, the offence became confined to threats to public order, but it was still invoked against those who sought to alter our system of government.

---

20 The offences of seditious, defamatory and obscene libel were abolished by the Coroners and Justice Act 2009, section 73.

21 See Edward P. Cheyney, 'The Court of Star Chamber', *The American Historical Review*, 18(4), July 1913, pp. 727–50.

In 1792, Thomas Paine was convicted for publishing a seditious libel on the ground that his work, *The Rights of Man*, had brought the King into hatred and contempt. In 1909, Guy Aldred, a Glaswegian anarchist, was tried at the Old Bailey for publishing an article in the *Indian Sociologist* advocating the end of colonialism.[22] It described the execution of an Indian Nationalist as an act of murder by 'the lick-spittle crew of Imperialistic bloodsucking, capitalist parasites'. It glorified an Indian student who had been executed for murder as a martyr for Indian independence. The judge directed the jury that the truth of what was written was not a defence and nor was the writer's innocence of motive. Aldred was sentenced to twelve months' hard labour.

Critics of those in power in Commonwealth Asia risk similar treatment today. In 2012, Aseem Trivedi, an Indian political cartoonist, was charged with sedition for publishing cartoons criticising corruption. The charges were later dropped following a public outcry – but the crime lingers and the threat of its use chills political debate. In Malaysia in 2000, the former Vice President of the National Justice Party was charged with sedition. He had claimed that the ruling party had incited massacres of ethnic Chinese during the Sino-Malay violence in 1969.

Though seditious libel was abolished in the UK in 2009, its ghost still haunts our system. Free speech and academic freedom are not sufficiently valued by our governors. In 2014, the government included a provision, known as the 'Prevent' policy, in a Counter-Terrorism Bill. 'Prevent' placed universities, local authorities, prison officers, schools and hospitals under a duty to have regard 'to the need to prevent people from being drawn into terrorism'. The Home Office envisaged that duty as involving banning 'extremist' views from campus, even if they were

---

22 *R v Aldred* (1909) 22 Cox CC 1.

non-violent and even though the criminal law already protects against incitement to hatred as well as violence. The links between non-violent (as opposed to violent) extremism and terrorism are neither direct nor obvious. The government was forced to drop some of those plans in the face of opposition from Liberal Democrats and the House of Lords.[23] But we were unable to exempt higher education institutions from the duty altogether,[24] or to change the broad definition of 'extremism', which captures anything that constitutes 'vocal or active opposition to fundamental British values'.

The notion of 'fundamental British values' implies that there are values uniquely cherished in this country as part of being 'British'. But we have no written constitution or other code defining 'British values'. The Human Rights Act embodies values – but they are universal, not especially 'British', shared by the rest of democratic Europe and beyond. Any attempt to define extremism as involving opposition to vague British values runs the risk that those who strongly disagree with the government and its actions will be treated as 'un-British' and subversive, perhaps guilty of misconduct akin to treason.

Extremism flourishes in all communities – but fear of 'the other' may lead our governors to concentrate unduly on extremism in communities with which they do not identify. The Independent Reviewer of Terrorism Legislation, David Anderson QC, has rightly cautioned that:

---

23 The Counter-Terrorism and Security Act 2015 (Risk of Being Drawn into Terrorism) (Amendment and Guidance) Regulations 2015 were approved by the House of Lords on 17 September 2015.
24 HL Deb 4 February 2015, vol. 759, c. 667; HL Deb 9 February 2015, vol. 759, cols. 1024–1034.

Any fair-minded person will see that if violent Islamist extremism is a fair target, so too must be violent neo-Nazi extremism. But active opposition to freedom of expression . . . is easier to condone, or not to notice, when it comes from one's own community. Thus, Muslims who engage in non-violent protest against insulting depictions of the prophet meet the . . . definition of extremism . . . Yet few would think of categorising as extremists those who urge the prosecution of Muslims for insulting the war dead by burning poppies on Armistice Day (indeed 82% of Britons approved of such prosecutions in 2011).[25]

There are already reports of such targeting. One postgraduate student at Staffordshire University was accused of being a potential terrorist – because a university official had spotted him reading a textbook in the college library entitled *Terrorism Studies*. Mohammed Umar Farooq was enrolled in the terrorism, crime and global security master's programme. He was reportedly questioned about attitudes to homosexuality, Islamic State and al Qaeda.[26] The university subsequently apologised to Farooq and admitted that the incident had exposed the difficulties in implementing the government's 'Prevent' policy.

We have been here before, during the 'Troubles' in Northern Ireland. In October 1988, after a heightened period of violence, Margaret Thatcher's government decided to starve the IRA and

---

25 David Anderson QC, *The Terrorism Acts in 2014: Report of the Independent Reviewer on the Operation of the Terrorism Act 2000 and Part 1 of the Terrorism Act 2006*, September 2015, pp. 58–59, §9.16. Anderson is citing *Redmond-Bate v DPP* [1999] EWHC Admin 732, *per* Lord Justice Sedley. Italics have been removed from the original source.
26 Randeep Ramesh and Josh Halliday, 'Student accused of being a terrorist for reading book on terrorism', *Guardian*, 28 September 2015.

Sinn Féin of what she described as 'the oxygen of publicity'.[27] The Home Secretary banned the media from broadcasting any interviews with people from designated terrorist organisations. The ban was limited to direct speech, so journalists circumvented it by showing interviews with actors dubbed over the top. The dubbing was farcical. It provided some entertainment, a focus for grievance by Republican groups and a reason to ridicule the government. But it is doubtful that it made terrorism less likely or weakened the IRA. On the contrary, it had the opposite effect: political support for Republicanism increased across Ireland.[28]

Now unrestrained by a coalition partner, the Home Secretary, Theresa May, seeks a new law granting her the power to ban extremist organisations even if they are non-violent – like Hizb ut-Tahrir, an international pan-Islamic organisation that seeks an Islamic state by non-violent means. Banning orders would be reinforced by extremism disruption orders and closure orders, and there would be attempts to restrict extremist views on social media. Legislation against 'extremism' could encourage disaffection among young British Muslims and political witch hunts reminiscent of Senator Joe McCarthy's pursuit in the early 1950s of those he accused of 'un-American' activities. For what

---

27 I was counsel with David Pannick in an unsuccessful challenge to the ban: R (Brind) v Secretary for the Home Department [1991] 1 AC 696 (HL).

28 Northern Ireland's government had attempted even more draconian restrictions in the 1970s. In 1971, Dublin banned Northern Ireland's state broadcaster, the RTE, from allowing spokespersons of the IRA on air. In 1976, it strengthened the ban so that the RTE could not interview a Sinn Féin speaker under any circumstances – even on a subject unrelated to the campaign of violence in Northern Ireland. It also tried to extend censorship to newspapers.

is opposition to 'British values,' other than a display of 'un-British values'? Bad ideas are ultimately defeated by argument, not censorship. Free speech is a basic 'British' value. The government's aim of preventing extremism must respect it.

Blasphemy

In 2008, Parliament abolished the common law offence of blasphemous libel,[29] which prohibited attacks on the Christian religion.[30] The offence had been infamously used in 1922, when John William Gott was convicted and sentenced to a year's imprisonment with hard labour for having sold two pamphlets at a market in Stratford Broadway. One described Jesus Christ entering Jerusalem 'like a circus clown on the back of two donkeys'.[31] Gott was a very sick man – but the Home Secretary refused to set him free on compassionate grounds.

After Gott's case, no one had been prosecuted for blasphemy until 1977, when Mary Whitehouse, the fierce opponent of the permissive society, brought a private prosecution against the publishers of *Gay News*. She was offended by a homoerotic poem entitled 'The love that dares not speak its name' about a homosexual centurion's sexual encounter with Christ at the Crucifixion. The jury gave a ten-to-two guilty verdict.

---

29 Section 79 Criminal Justice and Immigration Act 2008 (applicable only in England and Wales). The Northern Ireland government has not been willing to abolish the offence, even though Northern Ireland has a separate law dealing with incitement to religious hatred.

30 *R (on the application of Green) v City of Westminster Magistrates' Court* [2007] EWHC 2785 (Admin).

31 *R v Gott* (1922) 16 Cr App Rep 87.

On appeal, the Law Lords could have declared the offence obsolete. Instead, they breathed new life into it.[32] Lord Scarman even recommended that it be extended to protect the religious beliefs and feelings of non-Christians.

Scarman's unwise suggestion was taken up in 1991, when a British Muslim, Abdul Hussain Choudhury, tried to bring a private prosecution against Salman Rushdie and Viking Penguin for publishing *The Satanic Verses*. Mr Choudhury argued that what had been good law in eighteenth-century England to defend Christianity should these days protect Islam. He referred the court to the punishments advocated in the Qur'an, including amputations and stoning to death. Lord Justice Tasker Watkins dryly pointed out that it didn't 'leave much room for probation in your system'.

I represented Viking Penguin. We persuaded the court that it would be divisive to extend the offence.[33] We argued that one person's religious belief is blasphemy to a follower of another belief – for example, whether the Messiah has come (Christian) or is still to come (Jewish).

Muslims around the world held protests about the book's depiction of the Prophet and it was banned in several countries. The Supreme Leader of Iran, Ayatollah Khomeini, issued a *fatwa* calling for Rushdie to be murdered – along with the book's editors and publishers. He declared that the murderer would be a martyr.

The Union of Islamic Students' Associations in Europe issued a statement offering its services to Ayatollah Khomeini. The founding Secretary General of the Muslim Council of Britain was reported to have said that 'death was too easy for Rushdie'

---

32 *Whitehouse v Gay News Ltd, R v Lemon* [1979] AC 617 (HL).
33 *R v Metropolitan Chief Magistrate, ex p. Choudhury* [1991] 1 QB 429 (DC).

– instead, his mind ought to be 'tormented for the rest of his life unless he asks for forgiveness to Almighty Allah.'[34] Rushdie had to go into hiding to escape the *fatwa*.

Although Parliament finally abolished the crime of blasphemy in 2008, its legacy continues to infect countries of the former British Empire. English blasphemy law was written into the Indian Penal Code in 1860. It remains in force there and elsewhere in parts of Asia that Britain used to rule. It has led to terrible crimes committed in the name of God and religion.

Pakistan inherited the Penal Code and added an offence for using derogatory remarks about the Prophet, punishable by the death penalty. It also forbids members of a non-orthodox Muslim movement, Ahmadi Muslims, from calling their places of worship mosques, or performing any act that outrages the feelings of other Muslims. These and other speech crimes are invoked to settle personal vendettas and as a cover for persecuting religious minorities. They are enforced by mob rule, murder and intimidation.

In 2009, Aasia Bibi was found guilty of insulting Islam and the Prophet and sentenced to death by hanging. She is an illiterate mother of five. Events leading to her so-called 'crime' began with a quarrel over a bowl of water. Near a village in the Punjab province in Pakistan, a group of female farm workers were suffering from the heat. Mrs Bibi offered them water but was rebuffed. She was a Christian, they said, and therefore her water was unclean. Rather than swallowing the indignity, she defended her faith and was alleged to have insulted the Prophet and Islam. The local mullah called on his followers to take

---

34 Peter Murtagh, 'Rushdie in hiding after Ayatollah's death threat', *Guardian*, 18 February 1989.

action against her. A mob pursued her until the police took her into custody.[35]

The Imam of Peshawar's oldest mosque, Maulana Yousaf Qureshi, offered a reward for anyone who killed her. His call to violence was endorsed by *Nawa-i-Waqt*, Pakistan's second largest-selling newspaper. The Governor of Punjab urged her release and was assassinated. Fanatics hailed his killer as a hero and showered him with petals when he left court. The Minister for Minorities, Shahbaz Bhatti, advocated the repeal of Pakistan's blasphemy laws. He was the only Christian member of the government. He was threatened with beheading, then shot dead in 2011.

In 2012, a Pakistani academic, Muhammad Shakil Auj, delivered a speech in the USA in which he argued that Muslim women ought to be allowed to marry non-Muslim men. He was the Dean of Islamic Studies at the University of Karachi and a well-known liberal. He was accused of blasphemy and shot and killed in Karachi in September 2014 by unknown attackers. Another visiting religious scholar at the same Islamic Studies department, Maulana Masood Baig, was also shot dead.

In Bangladesh, the government banned a novel by Taslima Nasrin about the persecution of Hindus, called *Lajja* (*Shame*). Militant Islamist groups put a bounty on her head. She fled to Europe. When she published the first volume of her autobiography, the Bangladeshi government banned the book and ordered the police to seize all copies of the second volume. She was tried in her absence and sentenced to a year's imprisonment for 'derogatory remarks about Islam'.

------

35 She was sentenced to death by a district court. In July 2015 the Pakistiani Supreme Court stayed her sentence pending her legal appeal in the Pakistani High Court. Her husband has asked the British government to seek clemency for his wife.

Then in February 2015 an American blogger, Avijit Roy, was hacked to death with machetes by unidentified assailants in Dhaka. He was a secular humanist of Bangladeshi origin. His blog championed secular writing in Bangladesh.

The Organisation of Islamic Cooperation campaigns at the United Nations to create global laws criminalising insults to religion. If sanctioned by international law, they would be used to undermine individual rights and lend legitimacy to those who punish religious minorities, dissenters and non- believers.

Religious offences are not confined to Muslim countries. Vladimir Putin used blasphemy laws to jail Pussy Riot, a punk band. European Jewish leaders, backed by EU heads of state, have called for Europe-wide legislation outlawing anti-Semitism, Holocaust denial and other activities deemed to violate religious rights.[36] The Irish Constitution too proscribes blasphemy. To give effect to it, Ireland passed a Defamation Act in 2009, creating a new offence of 'publication or utterance of blasphemous matter' that is 'grossly abusive or insulting in relation to matters held sacred by any religion'.[37] There have been no prosecutions but its presence in Irish law is an embarrassment. At the UN Human Rights Council in 2009, Pakistan proposed adopting its precise wording. The Irish government intended to seek approval for its repeal in a referendum – but backtracked. Across the world the struggle for and against free expression between the followers of different religions (or lack of them) will continue. It would be hazardous to predict the outcome.

---

36 Ian Traynor, 'Jewish leaders call for Europe-wide legislation outlawing antisemitism', *Guardian*, 25 January 2015.
37 Henry McDonald, 'Dawkins among atheists urging Irish PM to hold blasphemy law referendum', *Guardian*, 11 February 2015.

The right to offend

Blasphemy is not the only over-broad crime against offensive speech. In 2013, Parliament abolished the offence of using 'insulting' words or behaviour in a way that harms public order.[38] The offence had been used to arrest or prosecute religious campaigners against homosexuality, a British National Party member who displayed anti-Islamic posters in his window, and people who swore at the police.

There is a right (but not a duty) to offend. In the words of the Strasbourg Court, the right to freedom of expression applies not only to information and ideas:

> That are favourably received or regarded as inoffensive or as a matter of indifference, but also to those that offend, shock or disturb the State or any sector of the population. Such are the demands of that pluralism, tolerance and broadmindedness without which there is no 'democratic society'.[39]

The law of the American Constitution allows too much protection to hate speech. It allows suppression only when violence or violation of law is intended and likely to take place imminently. The test of imminence is too narrow. That is why Pastor Terry Jones could not be prevented or punished for publicly burning copies of the Qur'an in Florida in the certain knowledge that it would produce violence across the Muslim world.

---

38 Section 57 Crime and Courts Act 2013.
39 *Handyside v United Kingdom* (1976) 1 EHRR 737, §49. That statement of principle about the right to offend echoed Justice Holmes's reference in the American Supreme Court to 'freedom for the thought that we hate' (Dissenting in *United States v Schwimmer*, 279 US 644 (1929)).

The right to offend is the price of free expression in a liberal democracy. Nowhere was this principle clearer than in the global outcry at the barbaric murders at the offices of *Charlie Hebdo* magazine in February 2015. On the evening of the attacks, crowds of thousands gathered spontaneously in Paris, Toulouse, Lyon, Marseille, Nantes and Rennes, holding up plac-ards with the phrase 'Je suis Charlie'. The slogan quickly rose to the top of Twitter hashtags worldwide.

Charlie Hebdo has published many irreverent and deliberately offensive cartoons. It has blasphemed all faiths and derided politics and popular culture as well as religion. It has mocked the African sex slaves of Boko Haram. It once depicted the Father, the Son and the Holy Ghost in a sexual threesome. It satirised the oppression of women under Sharia law and published cartoons of bullet-ridden Qur'ans. It portrayed the Prophet in degrading positions – once nude, once hiding a bomb in his turban. The Jihadists reportedly shouted 'Allahu akbar' ('God is great') after they gunned down nine of the magazine's staff, a maintenance worker and two police officers.

Cartoons should enjoy no immunity from criminal prosecu-tion if they are deliberately intended to stir up violence and likely to have that effect, even if violence is not imminent. Drawings can be as powerful as *Mein Kampf*. The Nazi leader Julius Streicher is infamous because his virulent anti-Semitic magazine *Der Stürmer* published cartoons portraying Jews as blood-sucking demons. That is why many Jews support strong race and religious hate speech crimes. I understand their concerns but they go too far in seeking to forbid free speech that causes them justifiable offence. The same is true for Muslims and Christians who press to limit insulting speech.

Many Muslims feel strongly that it should be a serious crime to insult the Prophet and Islam, along the lines of the old law of blasphemy. The Muslim Council of Britain pressed the Blair government to make religious hate speech a crime. New Labour feared that the invasion of Iraq in 2003 would lose them electoral support among British Muslims. The Home Secretary promised mosque leaders that if their followers supported Labour, the government would introduce the legislation they wanted. It kept that promise after winning the General Election in 2004 by bringing in a Racial and Religious Hatred Bill to forbid incitement against members of a religious group.

The proposals swept too broadly. They covered insults as well as threats. The government denied that the Bill would interfere with free speech. Rowan Atkinson, the comic actor, spoke convincingly against it:

> To criticise a person for their race is manifestly irrational and ridiculous but to criticise their religion, that is a right . . . The freedom to criticise ideas, any ideas – even if they are sincerely held beliefs – is one of the fundamental freedoms of society and a law which attempts to say you can criticise and ridicule ideas as long as they are not religious ideas is a very peculiar law indeed.[40]

The Bill was vigorously criticised by writers and entertainers, as well as by both main opposition parties and conservative Protestant groups. I drafted a clause to draw its sting. It made the crime harmless and unenforceable by guaranteeing that it would not restrict criticism and expressions of 'antipathy, dislike, ridicule, insult or abuse of particular religions or the beliefs or

---

40 Toby Helm, 'Atkinson defends right to offend', *Telegraph*, 7 December 2004.

practices of their adherents'.[41] It was passed with overwhelming support in the Lords and squeaked through the Commons.[42]

Libel law reform

English libel law, developed by the courts over centuries, was notoriously oppressive. It favoured the protection of the reputation of the rich and powerful, who used it to deter criticism and obtain exorbitant jury awards of damages. The rich and powerful were the only ones who could afford the cost of bringing an action.

Claimants did not have to show that the defamatory words caused them any loss or harm. Citizen critics and small media outlets self-censored or settled for fear their business could be ruined by the heady sums involved in litigation. The law's bias in favour of reputation encouraged 'libel tourism' – wealthy foreign claimants suing in London for libels that had little connection with England.

Dr Rachel Ehrenfeld was one well-known victim. In 2003, she wrote a book called *Funding Evil: How Terrorism is Financed – and How to Stop It*. It made serious allegations against the Saudi billionaire Khalid bin Mahfouz, alleging that he had channelled money to al Qaeda. It was published in hard copy in New York and one chapter was put online. Only twenty-three copies were sold in Britain via the internet, but Mr Mahfouz and his two sons

---

41 The Racial and Religious Hatred Act 2006, schedule 1. The Public Order Act has also been amended to criminalise incitement to race and homophobic hatred. It is unfair that the law protects more strongly against race hate speech than homophobic hate speech. When I made this argument in the House of Lords and tried to amend the law, however, I was defeated.

42 Parliament also amended the Bill to confine the offences to threatening words and place the burden on the prosecution to prove specific intent.

sued successfully in London. Rachel Ehrenfeld was ordered to pay damages and legal costs totalling £110,000. The case provoked an outcry in the United States. President Obama gave his approval to an Act of Congress – known as the SPEECH Act[43] – which made UK libel judgments unenforceable in the United States as incompatible with American constitutional values.

In 2009, a coalition of free speech NGOs published a report entitled *Free Speech Is Not for Sale*, recommending wholesale reform. There was cross-party support for it. I decided to introduce a Private Member's Bill, helped by an advisory group of legal experts, free speech NGOs and a parliamentary drafter. We identified practical reforms that would have a good chance of becoming law.

We considered how the law should protect so-called 'political speech'. One way involved barring 'public figures' from claiming for libel unless the damage to their reputation was malicious.[44] That is the position in the United States[45] – but it had no hope of

---

43 Securing the Protection of our Established and Enduring Constitutional Heritage Act (SPEECH Act).

44 'Malicious' is understood to mean that the libel was published intentionally or with reckless disregard for truth.

45 The US position is known as the *Sullivan* rule, from *New York Times v Sullivan*, 376 US 254 (1964). The case approved a judgment of the Supreme Court of Illinois in *City of Chicago v Tribune Co.* (1923) 139 NE 86. Where the claimant is a 'public figure' (a politician or celebrity who is a household name), an action for libel will not be possible unless there is proof by clear and convincing evidence that the defendant published the statement with knowledge of its falsity or in reckless disregard of its truth or falsity. See generally, Anthony Lewis, *Make No Law: The Sullivan Case and the First Amendment* (New York: Vintage Books, 1992). There are objections in principle about the way the *Sullivan* rule has been extended by the Supreme Court (see Lester, 'Two Cheers for the First Amendment', *Harvard Law and Policy Review*, 8(1), 2014, pp. 177–94).

being approved by Parliament. It would have involved politicians restricting their own powers to sue – turkeys being asked to vote for Christmas.

Instead, we decided to give the courts the power to strike out trivial libel claims at an early stage unless the claimant could show they had suffered serious harm. To protect responsible journalism, we devised a defence of responsible publication on matters of public interest.[46]

We also updated the law to cover defamation via the internet. The old law meant that every time a defamatory statement was repeated – each time a book or newspaper was read, each time someone watched a television programme or listened to a radio broadcast – it gave rise to a fresh claim.[47] That meant that each new click on a web page, every email forwarded and each comment 'shared' or 're-tweeted' gave rise to a new cause of action. We created a new 'single publication' rule to limit liability.

That was the easier part. A more difficult problem relates to the responsibility of website operators for defamation by website users. When defamatory comments are written under a news article or by users of social media, for example, the website hosts may not be aware of them. But it is often difficult to trace the

---

46 This was a user-friendly defence that replaced the one set out by the Law Lords in the *Reynolds* case (mentioned earlier in the chapter).

47 The multiple publication rule came from the *Duke of Brunswick*'s case (*Brunswick v Harmer* (1849) 14 QB 185). *The Times* failed to persuade the Court of Appeal or the Strasbourg Court that the multiple publication rule should be abandoned at least for statements published via the internet, so as to remove the problem of online publishers being exposed indefinitely to the risk of defamation actions across the world (*Times Newspapers Ltd v United Kingdom (Nos. 1 and 2)* [2009] ECHR 451 and *Loutchansky v Times Newspapers Ltd (Nos. 2–5)* [2001] EWCA Civ 1805).

person who wrote the defamatory comment. We needed to provide claimants with an effective way of dealing with defamatory allegations made online, while giving some protection to website operators. We created a new defence to libel where a website operator could show that they had not posted the statement. But it would be available only to a website operator who responds adequately to complaints about a defamatory posting – for example, by putting the claimant in touch with the poster, or (having been unsuccessful at finding and notifying the poster) by taking down the post.[48]

Another controversial issue was whether companies should be able to sue for libel. Rich companies regularly threaten publishers with baseless libel proceedings to intimidate them and thereby suppress criticism. Unlike individuals, companies do not have feelings that may be hurt by a libel. On the other hand, not all companies are rich. It would be unfair and discriminatory to treat them all in the same way. We decided that companies should be able to sue – but only if they could show reputational damage in the form of substantial financial loss.

The Bill was ready to be introduced immediately after the 2010 General Election. The coalition government and the Labour opposition were committed to reform. The Ministry of Justice undertook a public consultation and published its own draft Bill, drawing on our ideas. The government Bill won wide favour – except from libel lawyers whose livelihood would be affected and politicians with grievances against the press.

---

48 Section 5 Defamation Act 2013 sets out the defence, while the Defamation (Operators of Website) Regulations 2013 details the new process for making and responding to complaints about defamatory third party postings.

After much scrutiny and debate the Defamation Act became law in England and Wales on 25 April 2013. It strikes a fair balance between free speech and the protection of a good reputation. But the governments of Northern Ireland and Scotland refused to apply it to their countries.[49] As a result, there is weaker protection of freedom of speech and the press in Northern Ireland and Scotland than in England and Wales. Publishers have to comply with different legal standards across the UK. That would not happen if freedom of expression were protected by uniform constitutional standards, as in federal countries, such as the USA, Canada and Germany. It is a deeply unsatisfactory situation, but the government insists that it is helpless to intervene.

Freedom of information

Milton, Paine and J.S. Mill sought above all to protect opinions – especially those of political and religious dissenters. They were not concerned with the free flow of *information*. It is only recently that a positive right of access to information held by public bodies has developed in many democracies. It remains unwelcome to governments addicted to secrecy with an aversion to openness. Excessive government secrecy undermines the ability to hold government to account. The control of access to information is a powerful weapon in the hands of our political masters.

---

49 In 2015, the Northern Irish Law Commission held a consultation on extending the Defamation Act to Northern Ireland. This closed in February 2015, and the Commission was closed down a month later. At the time of publication, responsibility for the report has passed to the Department of Finance.

In December 1997, Tony Blair's New Labour government published a White Paper with the title *Your Right to Know – Freedom of Information*. The introduction explained that:

> Unnecessary secrecy in government leads to arrogance in governance and defective decision-making. The perception of excessive secrecy has become a corrosive influence in the decline of public confidence in government.[50]

The Prime Minister wrote that the government's intention was to break down the 'traditional culture of secrecy' and to 'give people in the United Kingdom the legal right to know'. The ministerial architect of the White Paper, David Clark MP, wrote that openness was 'fundamental to the political health of a modern state' and promised that the new law would:

> Mark a watershed in the relations between the government and the people of the United Kingdom. At last there is a government ready to trust the people with a legal right to information. This right is central to a mature democracy.

Fine words but they were not the views of the Prime Minister. It is political insincerity as much as excessive secrecy that has corroded public confidence in those to whom we entrust power. Tony Blair wrote in his autobiography that his promise of a Freedom of Information (FOI) Act made him an 'idiot . . . naïve, foolish, irresponsible nincompoop'. He removed the liberally minded David Clark and replaced him with Jack Straw, who boasted in his memoir of his role as 'villain of the piece' in

---

50 Cabinet Office, *Your Right to Know – Freedom of Information*, Cm 3818, 11 December 1997.

scuttling his government's original proposals and producing an emasculated version.[51]

We Liberal Democrats fought to strengthen the Bill during its passage in the Lords. But we were warned that unless we gave in, the government would pull the Bill. The government was not bluffing, so we reluctantly decided that half a loaf was better than no bread. Even then, Jack Straw managed to weaken the Bill and delay the coming into force of the FOI Act for five years.

The FOI Act contains unnecessary escape clauses. There are absolute exemptions for information relating to the security and intelligence services, and for any information about Parliament that the Speaker of the Commons decides to keep confidential.[52] There is an exemption for information whose release could prejudice the 'effective conduct of public affairs'. There is also another to protect commercial interests – a popular excuse for refusing to scrutinise how private companies contracted by governments spend taxpayer money. Those conducting public inquiries can also refuse information requests without giving reasons – even when the information is of great public interest and might expose the abuse of power.[53]

---

51 Jack Straw, *Last Man Standing: Memoirs of a Political Survivor* (London: Macmillan, 2012), pp. 277–82.
52 Sections 23 and 34 Freedom of Information Act 2000.
53 Section 32(2) Freedom of Information Act 2000. See *Kennedy v Charity Commission* [2014] UKSC 20. A majority suggested a common law alternative way of obtaining the information by means of judicial review. Dominic Kennedy and Times Newspapers Ltd have complained to the Strasbourg Court of breaches of their right to freedom of expression under Article 10 of the Convention. The application is pending and the author acts for the applicants.

Yet for all its flaws the Act has great value in protecting the public's right to know. It created a right to disclosure and a framework for striking a balance between different aspects of the public interest. It enabled the public to find out that prison authorities were using techniques designed to control young prisoners – some children as young as twelve – by inflicting pain through strikes to their faces, ribs and groins. Disclosures about the National Health Service exposed failures to respond to serious threats to patient safety, unacceptable delays, overstretched casualty units and a disparity in surgery-related death rates across different hospitals.[54] In 2013, the Act helped reveal that one thousand care home residents had suffered dehydration-related deaths between 2003 and 2012, suggesting elderly or vulnerable patients had been left without enough water. A disclosure from the Department for Work and Pensions showed that the government's tax and benefits policy was estimated to push two hundred thousand children into absolute poverty.

The FOI Act is not popular with politicians, especially those in power or with embarrassing secrets to hide. When a journalist, Heather Brooke, was working on a book called *Your Right to Know*,[55] she filed requests seeking a breakdown of the expenses claimed by MPs. She was initially refused access but eventually succeeded when she appealed the decision before the Information Tribunal, which described the Commons system as 'a recipe for confusion, inconsistency and the risk of misuse'.[56]

---

54 Examples taken from the report by Campaign for Freedom of Information, *Disclosures under the FOI Act*, January 2014.
55 Heather Brooke, *Your Right to Know: A Citizen's Guide to the Freedom of Information Act* (London: Pluto Press, 2006).
56 *Corporate Officer of the House of Commons v Information Commissioner* [2008] 3 All ER 403, §14.

The Commons authorities sought to prevent her accessing the information – but the High Court ruled that MPs' expenditure of public money was 'a matter of direct and reasonable interest to taxpayers' and that the system lacked transparency and accountability.

Instead of publishing information about MPs' receipts, the Commons tried a different tactic: to persuade Parliament to amend the Act to exempt themselves from it. It was a classic example of institutional bias – being judges in their own cause. In 2007, David Maclean, a former Conservative Minister and Chief Whip, introduced a Bill to amend the Act by exempting both the House of Commons and the House of Lords from it and preventing disclosure of all communications between MPs and the public. The government unofficially supported it. It was rushed through the Commons and sent to the Lords. To the great credit of the House of Lords, not a single Peer was willing to sponsor the Bill.

In his memoir Tony Blair criticised the fact that the FOI Act is used for the most part by journalists rather than by 'the people'.[57] But it is the crucial role of the press in a modern participatory democracy to act as a public watchdog alerting and informing the public about matters of public interest.

In Jack Straw's view, the Act has:

Made good decision-making more difficult . . . degrading of the historical record more likely . . . [and has not] increased trust in government, as its proponents promised.[58]

---

57 Tony Blair, *A Journey* (London: Hutchinson, 2010), p. 517.
58 Jack Straw, *Last Man Standing: Memoirs of a Political Survivor* (London: Macmillan, 2012), p. 287.

The public's lack of trust in politicians is not the fault of the FOI Act but of politicians' abuse of public trust and their attempts to conceal from the public information that should be public property. They have failed to meet the standards we expect of those in public life.

In 2015, the Supreme Court decided that communications between Prince Charles and government ministers should be released under the Act. The Prince had written twenty-seven letters to various government departments and a *Guardian* journalist had asked to see them. The Attorney General refused. He said that the correspondence contained the Prince's 'most deeply held personal views and beliefs' and disclosure might undermine his 'position of political neutrality', which he might not be able to recover from when king. Prince Charles has a right to his beliefs and a right to campaign and lobby, like everyone else. But not everyone has an open line to ministers. If he advances a political agenda then the public surely has a right to know.

The FOI Act has failed to drive out the culture of secrecy that still infects Whitehall and has been espoused by senior Conservative and Labour ministers and civil servants. I know of no examples of good governance being damaged by more open government. The cost to central government departments in complying with the Act is fifty times less than the external communications budget.[59] But the FOI Act is currently under threat from the Prime Minister and his government.

---

59 Central government departments spend less than £6 million a year answering FOI requests – around 0.001% of the £577.4 billion the central government spent in the 2015 fiscal year. The Government Communication Service estimated its spending on external communications activities in 2014–15 at £289 million. 'Cost to central Government of complying with FoI 50 times less than external comms budget', *Legal Gazette*, 13 October 2015.

In July 2015, David Cameron appointed an independent panel to assess whether the Act is maintaining the right balance between transparency and 'the need for sensitive information to have robust protection'.[60] It was chaired by a former senior Treasury civil servant and included Jack Straw, the reluctant architect and strong critic of the FOI Act. It considered whether to strengthen the powers of ministers to veto the release of information to the public and whether to charge for FOI requests – measures with grave implications for transparency and openness in government. The panel's final report rejected both suggestions. But we are yet to see how the Government will respond. The burden is on those who seek to narrow the Act. It is important we resist any weakening and fight to remove the unnecessary loopholes that undermine the legislation.

A culture of liberty

Freedom of opinion and freedom of expression are the foundation for every free and democratic society. Free expression is a necessary condition to realise the principles of transparency and accountability we need to protect human rights. It is the basis for the full enjoyment of many other human rights, such as freedom of assembly and association and the right to vote.

No law and no court can save our right to free speech without the support of a strong, popular culture of liberty. As Justice Brandeis observed long ago, 'the greatest menace to freedom is an inert people'.[61] Our courts have recognised that there is a

---

60 Written statement to Parliament, *Independent Commission on Freedom of Information*, 17 July 2015; Independent Commission on Freedom of Information, *Final Report*, 1 March 2016.
61 *Whitney v California* 274 US 357 (1927), p. 376.

right to freedom of expression protected by the common law. But we have no supreme written constitution limiting the powers of Parliament, and when the government of the day has a majority in the Commons it may enact repressive legislation beyond the reach of our courts. The Human Rights Act is the British alternative to a written constitution, backed where necessary by recourse to the European Court of Human Rights.

One of the greatest threats to free speech comes from the dogmatic intolerance of those who seek to impose their 'fighting faiths'[62] (whether political, religious or secular) on others. Their intolerance of what deeply offends them is divisive and corroding. Self-appointed campaigners have succeeded in closing down the performance of plays and exhibitions and banning books that offend them. Their campaigns encourage self-censorship. Their rights of protest and assembly are mistreated when they intimidate and abuse. We need to defend free expression against them as well as against censorship by the arms of the state: 'freedom for the thought that we hate'.[63]

---

62 The memorable phrase used by Justice Holmes in his celebrated dissenting judgment in *Abrams v United States* 250 US 616 (1919): 'Persecution for the expression of opinions seems to me perfectly logical. If you have no doubt of your premises or your power and want a certain result with all your heart you naturally express your wishes in law and sweep away all opposition . . . But when men have realised that time has upset many fighting faiths, they may come to believe even more than they believe the very foundations of their own conduct that the ultimate good desired is better reached by free trade in ideas . . . The best test of truth is the power of the thought to get itself accepted in the competition of the market, and that truth is the only ground upon which their wishes safely can be carried out.'

63 The title of Anthony Lewis's biography of the First Amendment (New York: Basic Books, 2009) borrowing the phrase of Justice Holmes Jr.

Our political masters would do well to heed the inscription on the main entrance to the Library of Congress in Washington DC, written by James Madison in August 1822:

A popular government, without popular information, or the means of acquiring it, is but a prologue to a Farce or a Tragedy; or, perhaps both. Knowledge will forever govern ignorance: And a people who mean to be their own Governors, must arm themselves with the power that knowledge brings.

4

PRIVACY

'With your permission you give us more information about you, your friends and we can improve the quality of our searches . . . We don't need you to type at all. We know where you are. We know where you've been. We can more or less know what you're thinking about.'
Eric Schmidt, CEO of Google (1 October 2010)

'The Party constantly watches all citizens for any sign of rebellion or thought-crime, but tries to appear kind and concerned rather than ruthless and invasive.'
George Orwell, *Nineteen Eighty-Four* (1949)

The right 'to respect for private and family life, home and correspondence' (as it is described in Article 8 of the European Convention on Human Rights) defies exhaustive definition. Its object is to protect the individual against unnecessary interference over a vast range of personal interests. They include respect for our personal identity, including our religious beliefs (or lack of them), our ethnicity, our gender and our sexual preferences. They also include respect for our psychological and physical integrity, when we make choices about medical treatment, or seek protection from unnecessary bodily searches. And they include respect for the confidentiality of private information – including our private correspondence and protection against unnecessary retention of fingerprints or DNA. The right to privacy also involves complex matters of life and death, including doctor-assisted suicide and decisions about whether or not to have a child, or to refuse life-sustaining medical treatment.

Privacy is essential to free thought, free choice and our relationships with others. Those who say 'if you've got nothing to hide, you've got nothing to fear' would surely mind if a stranger snooped over their shoulder as they wrote intimate emails, or stood in the corner of their bedroom watching them in bed. Protecting privacy means safeguarding against interference not just from public authorities, but private companies and members of professions, such as doctors, nurses and journalists.

Privacy and free speech jostle for protection. One difficult issue – highlighted by the Leveson report into the phone-hacking scandal – is how to maintain a fair balance between a free independent press and personal privacy. Another difficult issue involves how to balance privacy and national security (as well as the rule of law) in combatting terrorism and other serious crimes. Another set of difficult issues occurs when privacy rubs against professional expertise and ethics – when patients seek autonomy over their medical treatment or lack of it and their doctor disagrees with their choices. Sometimes that involves matters of life and death.

Judges as lawmakers

When British judges make the law they walk on tiptoes respecting Parliament as the supreme lawgiver. But because governments and Parliament have been reluctant to use their powers to legislate a right to privacy, it has been left to the judges for several hundred years to develop the law piecemeal.

In 1628, Chief Justice Coke coined the phrase 'a man's home is his castle'. A century and a half later, in 1774, Philip Stanhope, son of the Earl of Chesterfield, prevented a bookseller from publishing private letters written to him by his late father.[1] In 1849, a workman entrusted with Prince Albert and Queen Victoria's private etchings made surreptitious copies and sold them to a publisher. The court halted publication of a catalogue describing the etchings and ordered destruction of the copies.[2] The judge was moved by evidence that Queen Victoria found great pleasure from making the etchings in private. He wanted to protect the family from what the judge described as 'sordid spying into their domestic life'.

In 1889, Mr and Mrs Pollard stopped a photographer from selling Christmas cards containing Mrs Pollard's photograph. The photographer had displayed the cards in his shop window, whereas she had commissioned him to take the pictures for her private use. The court prevented him from committing a 'gross breach of faith'.[3]

That had been the piecemeal and haphazard development of this branch of English law when I began to practise at the English

---

1 *Thompson v Stanhope* (1774) 27 ER 476.
2 *Prince Albert v Strange* (1849) 64 ER 293.
3 *Pollard v Photographic Co* (1888) 40 Ch D 345.

Bar in 1964. I had studied the development of American privacy law at Harvard Law School, including the celebrated journal article by two Boston lawyers, Samuel D. Warren and Louis Brandeis. Drawing on English law, they argued that the time had come for the courts to recognise a right of privacy.[4] Some American state courts and legislatures did so.

I did not imagine that these academic forays would be useful at the English Bar. But then Margaret, Duchess of Argyll, came to my chambers, armed with leather-bound volumes of press cuttings about herself, each stamped with a ducal coronet. She wanted our help to persuade the courts to prevent her estranged husband, the Duke, from disclosing information about her in *The People* newspaper.[5] Angry at her adultery and in the throes of divorce proceedings, the Duke had taken her diaries, letters and photographs from her home in London and given them to the press.

We sought an order preventing public disclosure of marital confidences – 'the secrets of the marriage bed'. In truth there were few secrets of the marriage bed left after the salacious publicity given to her and her lovers in the divorce proceedings. But the legal principle was more important than the tiny amount of material excised by the judge from the newspaper. More importantly, the Duchess of Argyll's case was used (and misused) to develop a broader law protecting confidential information.[6]

---

4 Samuel D. Warren and Louis Brandeis, 'The Right to Privacy', *Harvard Law Review*, vol. 4, No. 5, 1890.
5 *Duchess of Argyll v Duke of Argyll* [1967] Ch 302.
6 I explained in the 'Free Speech' chapter how attempts were made to assert a public right to protect government privacy to prevent publication of Richard Crossman's *Diaries of a Cabinet Minister* and extracts from Peter Wright's *Spycatcher*.

The development of privacy protection was interrupted in 1979, when a senior judge – the Vice Chancellor, Sir Robert Megarry – declined to recognise a right of privacy in English law.[7] That case concerned James Malone, an antiques dealer with a dubious record. The police tapped his phone under a warrant issued by the Home Secretary. Mr Malone suspected that his phone calls and correspondence had been intercepted for several years. He went to court relying on the right to respect for his correspondence, protected by Article 8 of the European Convention on Human Rights.

The judge treated the Convention as irrelevant because Parliament had not made it part of English law. But he said that the control of telephone tapping was a subject that cried out for legislation, and expressed the hope that the Convention would 'provide a spur to action, however belated'.

It was a vain hope. The Home Secretary carried out a token review, and then announced that government would not be able to tap phones as effectively if subjected to oversight by the courts. The public should repose their trust in ministers, who would exercise the power responsibly.[8]

James Malone took his complaint to the European Court of Human Rights. It found that English law did not give the individual the legal protection required under the rule of law in a democratic society.[9] The UK had to fashion a law prescribing the scope and limits of police powers. The European Court explained that it was especially important to protect against arbitrary interference by public authorities when their power was exercised in secret.

---

7 *Malone v Metropolitan Police Commissioner* [1979] 1 Ch 344.
8 HC Deb 1 April 1980, vol. 982, cols. 205–207.
9 *Malone v United Kingdom* (1984) 7 EHRR 14.

In a limited and reluctant response, the government introduced the Interception of Communications Act in 1985. It covered interceptions using a public telephone but left out surveillance of other devices, private networks and metering.[10] The Bill was rightly described by Austin Mitchell MP as 'setting out to regulate canal traffic in the age of the high speed train and motorway'.[11]

A few years later, there were reports of gross press abuse of Russell Harty, host of an eponymous ITV chat show, as he lay in hospital dying of hepatitis. Journalists posed as junior doctors and demanded to see his medical records. Photographers had rented a flat opposite his hotel room from which to photograph him in bed.

When Gordon Kaye, a well-known actor and television star, lay in hospital recovering from brain surgery, a journalist and photographer from the *Sunday Sport* gained access to his room, interviewed him and took photos. The editor regarded the story as 'a great old fashioned scoop'.

Gordon Kaye's family tried to stop publication. It was the perfect case for the judiciary to recognise a right of privacy against media intrusion, but the Court of Appeal decided that it was a matter for Parliament and not the courts. It expressed the hope that 'the making good of this signal shortcoming in the law will not be long delayed'.[12] It was one of many futile hopes over decades of 'last chances' for the press barons and their editors.

---

10 'Metering' involves using a device to register telephone numbers dialled and the time and duration of each call – allowing the security services and the police to build up a picture of an individual's friends and contacts.

11 HC Deb 12 March 1985, vol. 75, col. 241.

12 *Kaye v Robertson* [1991] FSR 62 (CA), *per* Lord Justice Leggatt, p. 71.

A plague on Parliament and press

The political history of attempts to introduce privacy legislation and effective press regulation concerns decades of official procrastination and misplaced faith in the willingness of the press industry to reform itself. Successive governments have been reluctant to incur the wrath of newspaper owners and editors whose political support they seek.

The press rightly object to state institutions, including Parliament, being involved in their regulation. Journalists are the eyes and ears of the public. In a democratic society it is their function to expose misconduct in public office. The legitimate fear is that statutory regulation might one day be used as a way to cover up political scandals and stifle political debate, as happened in the medieval era under the Court of Star Chamber.[13] But effective regulation need not interfere with the vital independence of the press nor dampen debate on matters of public importance.

One of many failed attempts at tackling media abuse happened in 1970. The Home Secretary, Roy Jenkins, set up a Committee on Privacy chaired by a former Home Office Minister, Kenneth Younger. It received more complaints about the press than any other topic. Most were about harassment – journalists tracking down the subjects of their stories when they were on holiday, or phoning them in the middle of the night. Yet the Committee concluded that the standards of the press and broadcasting agencies had been improving and that the threat to privacy, far from growing, might even be diminishing.

---

13 The Licensing Order of 1643 was repressive. It gave rise to John Milton's *Areopagitica, A Speech for the Liberty of Unlicensed Printing* (1644).

Most members of the Younger Committee were opposed to enacting a privacy law. They felt that the courts were not well placed to decide the conflicts between privacy and free expression. They were also concerned that threat of a lawsuit for privacy intrusion might have a chilling effect, deterring journalists from publishing important stories in the public interest. The Younger Committee believed that if the press could self-regulate and editors acted with propriety, it would be better for free speech than legal restraint. It recommended improvements to the Press Council, a voluntary body set up by the press to deal with complaints about their conduct.[14]

News is a business and not only a profession. Commercial pressures push papers to publish salacious gossip and invasive stories. It is essential to ensure that those pressures do not drive newspapers to violate proper standards of journalism. But the Press Council lacked the power to do so. It could not provide effective remedies for victims of press abuse, such as ordering newspapers to compensate their victims or to print apologies.

In May 1974, the Wilson government set up a Royal Commission to inquire into editorial standards. It concluded that the case against unwarranted invasions of privacy by the press was 'overwhelming'. Like the Younger Committee, however, the Committee preferred reforming the Press Council to legislating a right to privacy and thereby allowing media invasions of privacy to be resolved by the courts.[15] It was concerned that the judicial route might have too chilling an effect on free expression. That disappointed Harold Wilson, who would have welcomed a privacy law.

---

14 *Report of the Committee on Privacy*, Cmnd 5012, 1972.
15 Royal Commission on the Press, *Final Report*, Cmnd 6810, 1977, §19.17–19.18.

Scandals involving press intrusion in the early 1980s sapped public confidence in the Press Council. In January 1981, the police arrested Peter Sutcliffe, the 'Yorkshire Ripper'. He was wanted for the murder of thirteen women and the attempted murder of seven others. Within forty-eight hours of Sutcliffe's arrest, journalists were pouring into Bradford and Dewsbury from all parts of Europe. Bids for the story of Sutcliffe's wife, Sonia, were pushed through the letterbox of her home. The *Daily Express* offered her £80,000; the *News of the World* offered £110,000. Sutcliffe's father and members of his family became guests of a newspaper in a Lancashire hotel.

Jacqueline Hill was the last of Sutcliffe's victims. She was a student, murdered in November 1980 at the age of twenty. Her mother heard of the offers of cash and began a campaign to stop the media offering huge pay-outs for interviews with Sutcliffe's friends and family.

In 1983, the Press Council investigated the vice of cheque book journalism. It expressed 'abhorrence and distaste' for enabling those connected to a criminal to profit from that connection and recommended that newspapers stop offering money for these interviews.[16] But it decided that a law against pay-outs was 'neither wholly desirable nor likely to prove practicable'. The House of Lords debated the report. Lord Harris of Greenwich, a former journalist and Home Office Minister, cautioned:

> In the circulation war now raging in Fleet Street between the tabloids in particular, in which the defeated will face extinction, a boost in circulation is regarded by some newspapers as far

---

16 Press Council, *Press Conduct in the Sutcliffe Case*, 1983, Chapter 15.

more important than a rap over the knuckles . . . If this process continues . . . there will be increasing demands that Parliament should take a hand . . . it is now time that the newspaper industry . . . put its own house in order.[17]

Lord Ardwick, former editor of *The Guardian* and adviser to the Mirror Group, said:

There is today among ordinary people a growing general ambivalence towards the media. The media are a Jekyll and Hyde. People are gripped by them and sometimes resent their own enslavement. They often feel that the papers, on the one side, and television, on the other, have become a two-headed monster with excessive power.[18]

David Mellor MP, the Minister responsible for media matters, appeared on Channel 4 and warned the press that they were 'drinking in the last chance saloon'.[19] He appointed a Committee, chaired by David Calcutt QC, to examine the case for a privacy law. Calcutt concluded that the press should have another 'final' chance to prove that voluntary self-regulation could be made to work. If they failed, Parliament would pass a law to set up a stronger regulator.[20]

The industry responded by creating a toothless Press Complaints Commission, the PCC, in 1991. It ignored some of

---

17 HL Deb, 20 July 1983, vol. 43, cols. 1164–1165.

18 HL Deb, 20 July 1983, vol. 43, cols. 1169–1170.

19 Channel 4, *Hard News*, 21 December 1989.

20 *Report of the Committee on Privacy and Related Matters*, Cm 1102, 1990. The Committee took the view that self-restraint by the press was a better way to secure respect for privacy 'in the context of a pre-eminent right to freedom of expression'.

Calcutt's recommendations and shelved others.[21] The PCC's members were picked by the industry and its Code of Practice was weak.[22]

That weakness of the PCC became clear when *The Sun* published the transcript of a private phone call between Princess Diana and her alleged lover. The Princess was in acrimonious pre-divorce proceedings with Prince Charles and during the call she expressed frustration with the royal family. *The Sun* set up a special phone line allowing thousands of callers to hear the thirty-minute recording for themselves, at thirty-six pence per minute. Not long afterwards, an Australian title published extracts of intimate conversations between Prince Charles and Camilla Parker Bowles, alluding to their sex life. British papers picked up the story. They were gross and gratuitous invasions of privacy – but the PCC took no public action.

In 1992, *The Scotsman* alleged that the then leader of the Liberal Democrats, Paddy Ashdown, had had an extramarital affair with his secretary. The information was obtained from a document stolen from his solicitor, so publication would have breached lawyer–client confidentiality. Ashdown had won an injunction to silence the story. But the ban extended only to titles in England and Wales and did not affect *The Scotsman*.

Again the PCC made no public comment. Its Chairman wrote a private letter to the Chairman of the Newspaper Association. He urged the media to practise self-restraint – not because of the value of preventing privacy intrusion *per se* – but

---

21 Lord Justice Leveson, *An Inquiry into the Culture, Practices and Ethics of the Press*, November 2012, Part D, Chapter 1, §6.1.
22 Sir David Calcutt QC, *Review of Press Self-Regulation*, Cm 2135, 1993.

because he worried that politicians would rally against the PCC.[23]

And when the PCC *did* berate newspapers, some behaved contemptuously. The *Daily Sport* printed two consecutive reports of sexual assault and included the names and other private details about the victims. When the PCC decided that the *Daily Sport* had breached the Code of Practice, it refused to print an apology.[24] In 1991, *The People* magazine published photos taken secretly of the baby daughter of the Duke and Duchess of York running naked in their garden. Even after receiving a complaint from her family, *The People* published the main picture again.[25]

After eighteen months of the PCC's operation, the government ordered another review by Calcutt. He concluded that the press was neither capable nor willing to initiate the reforms needed to prevent gross misbehaviour. He said it was now time for Parliament to step in and proposed statutory regulation of the press.

The PCC described the report as excessive. It agreed only to minor changes in its operation, to restrict eavesdropping and phone bugging. Regrettably, John Major's government bowed to the PCC's negative response. Another controversial story followed: the *Sunday Mirror* published photos of Princess Diana exercising in a private gym. When the PCC berated the paper, it responded not with contrition but by withdrawing from PCC oversight altogether.

---

23 Sir David Calcutt QC, *Review of Press Self-Regulation*, Cm 2135, 1993, §4.57–4.61.

24 Sir David Calcutt QC, *Review of Press Self-Regulation*, Cm 2135, 1993, §4.25–4.27.

25 Sir David Calcutt QC, *Review of Press Self-Regulation*, Cm 2135, 1993, §4.41.

When the Princess died in a car crash in Paris in 1997, the circumstances of her death reignited public anger at press misconduct. Her inebriated driver had been speeding to get away from the paparazzi. Editors made minor changes to their Code of Practice as a result – but much remained the same. The government and Parliament left the development of a privacy law to the courts, even though the Court of Appeal had made clear that it was a job for the legislature.[26]

Bringing privacy home

In 1997, Tony Blair's New Labour government introduced the Human Rights Bill. It enabled British courts to give effect to the rights protected by the European Convention on Human Rights – including both the right to free expression and the right to respect for privacy. I had campaigned for such a Bill for thirty years. As counsel representing newspapers, I had used the Convention on many occasions to protect press freedom. It had often come to their rescue, but British editors were unwilling to accept the other side of the coin – the need for safeguards against media intrusion on the private lives of public figures.

When the Human Rights Bill was introduced, a newspaper client asked me to try to persuade Parliament to give the press immunity from liability for invasions of privacy. I refused but (along with other newspapers) they attempted to convince Prime Minister Blair and Lord Chancellor Derry Irvine. Blair was apparently inclined to give the press what they wanted but Derry Irvine stood firm.

On the eve of the first Lords debate, the PCC's Chairman,

---

26 *Kaye v Robertson* [1991] FSR 62 (CA).

Lord Wakeham, warned in the *Mail on Sunday* that the Human Rights Bill would become a 'villains' charter' by introducing a privacy law through the back door. He claimed in the Lords that it would 'badly wound the system of tough and effective self-regulation that we have built up'.[27]

Derry Irvine explained that a privacy law developed by the courts would take account of the high value of the right to free expression. But the media barons would have none of it. Their editors have attacked the Human Rights Act and the European Court of Human Rights ever since, feeding the public with a diet of half-truths and downright lies.[28] Derry Irvine was hounded by sections of the press until Blair removed him from office in 2003.

Press abuse

In 2011, a disgraceful example of media abuse emerged. The *News of the World* had illegally hacked phones on a huge scale to retrieve private information for news stories. Its victims included former Prime Ministers, members of the royal family, celebrities, the relatives of deceased British soldiers, and the families of the victims of the 2005 London terrorist attacks. Its journalists had even hacked the voicemail of a murdered teenager, Milly Dowler, leading her family to the false hope that Milly might still be alive and accessing her messages.

David Cameron set up a public inquiry into phone hacking and police bribery by the *News of the World* and the wider culture and ethics of the British newspaper industry. The next day, it was announced that the paper would shut down, ending

---

27 HL Deb 24 November 1997, vol. 583, col. 771.
28 See the 'Human Rights' chapter.

168 years of publication. Two years later, in 2013, it emerged that the *Daily Mirror* and the *Sunday Mirror* had also been guilty of gross abuse, illegally hacking voicemails on an industrial scale.

The Leveson report was published in November 2012. It recognised that 'press freedom, hard won over three hundred years ago, should not be jeopardised' and that 'the press should not be delivered into the arms of the State'. But it also made damning findings of outrageous behaviour and recommended radical reforms to ensure that journalists would not abuse the right to free expression.

Among them, Leveson envisaged a new and far stronger press regulator. Though he was adamant the new regulator must be independent of politicians, Leveson thought it desirable to pass legislation to strong-arm the press into joining. If the press set up a regulator that met his criteria, any title that refused to join could face the threat of exemplary damages in court: inflated fines for breaking the law. And if the press refused to design a regulator that met Leveson's criteria, he suggested that they should be faced with Ofcom, the broadcasting regulator, as a 'backstop'. Ofcom is a statutory regulator and has far greater powers than have ever been used against the print media.

The Leveson report was politically toxic because of the love–hate relationship between politicians and journalists. They need each other and fear each other in equal measure. They are mutually dependent and yet proclaim their independence, each side claiming to represent the public interest better than the other. It is a world in which dog eats dog, and the public reputation of journalists and politicians is as low as it gets.

The three main political parties held talks that included the powerful lobby of the victims of press abuse, the celebrity-led Hacked Off group. They cobbled together a scheme to recognise the Leveson-style regulator. It was indirectly underpinned by legislation that threatened punitive damages against newspapers unwilling to join the system. The message to the press was that unless they submitted to the politicians' vision of how their regulator ought to behave, they could be punished in court. Publishers fear that if stirred by a controversial story – such as *The Daily Telegraph*'s revelations about the abuse of parliamentary expenses, or *The Guardian*'s exposure of surveillance malpractice – politicians might amend the scheme's design to impose draconian controls on the press.

The sanctions upon newspapers unwilling to join the system could violate the Convention right to free expression. They are unlikely to pass muster in the courts. There is nothing like it in any modern democracy and the politicians' scheme has been condemned internationally.

To work as envisaged, however, the scheme needs the press to cooperate by setting up a regulator that conforms to the politicians' framework. Instead, the press brought into being a rival regulator, the Independent Press Standards Organisation (IPSO). About ninety per cent of the industry instead lined up behind it.[29] IPSO does not conform to all of Leveson's recommendations but it is stronger and more powerful than the old PCC. It can fine the press up to £1 million, or one per cent of annual turnover. Its members are legally bound by its decisions.

Sir Alan Moses, a former Court of Appeal judge, chairs IPSO's

---

29 The *Financial Times* group opted out, *The Guardian* and *The Independent* remain undecided. They have devised their own in-house regulatory systems.

Board robustly. He made clear from the outset that he wanted to preserve Britain's 'free, fair and unruly press'. He also urged media proprietors to grant IPSO greater independence from them, because self-regulation should not mean the industry should 'mark its own exams'.[30]

As Sir Alan has pointed out,[31] IPSO could never command a consensus about the merits of its performance. Success in some quarters would involve the regulator slapping huge fines on newspapers on a daily basis. Success in others would mean standing back and allowing free expression to ride roughshod over all other components of the public interest. IPSO needs independent, transparent and accessible procedures to enable it to displease adherents of both extreme positions – press barons and Hacked Off.

The surveillance state

Gone are the days when we worried most about threats to privacy from nosy neighbours, CCTV cameras, wiretaps, journalists hiding in our garden hedges, or spies in the shadows. We are all digital addicts now – and we are all leaving digital tracks. We assume that MI5 and MI6 and GCHQ could track us if they needed to. Some of us trust them not to abuse their powers. Others do not. But then we have no alternative – except to break

---

30 Sir Alan Moses, *Speech at the Society of Editors' Annual Conference*, October 2014. In his view, greater independence could be achieved if the industry handed over control of the editors' Code of Practice to the regulator, and if IPSO were able to achieve long-term financial security.

31 Sir Alan Moses, *Evidence to the House of Lords Communications Committee*, 20 January 2015; *Speech at the Society of Editor's Annual Conference*, October 2014.

our machines or live as digital hermits. When broadband fails, we are bereft.

When George Orwell published *Nineteen Eighty-Four* in 1949, warning against dictatorship under 'Big Brother', he had in mind the totalitarian regimes of Hitler and Stalin and the risk of state power destroying free societies. That was long before the internet brought new opportunities for free expression across borders; long before private companies feasted on profits from harvesting our personal data; and long before the internet gave new surveillance capabilities to the friends and enemies of open society.

Search engines, email providers and social networking sites gather their customers' private data in enormous quantities. Many internet companies offer their services ostensibly for free – because they can sell our personal data to make money through advertising. We traded away our privacy without realising what we were giving up. Through analysis of buying patterns, a US retailer, Target, infamously predicted that one of its teenage customers was pregnant. It sent coupons for maternity wear through the letterbox – before she had broken the news to her parents.

Glenn Greenwald, the journalist best known for campaigning on internet privacy rights, complains of double standards. He reported that Eric Schmidt, CEO of Google, was asked in 2009 about the invasions of privacy that Google products were causing to hundreds of millions of people around the world. Schmidt responded that anyone doing something that they did not want others to know should not be doing it in the first place. In 2005, however, Schmidt allegedly banned Google employees from speaking with an online internet magazine, CNET. It had published an article full of private information about him – which it had obtained exclusively through using Google searches and other Google products.[32]

Tapping data from internet and telecoms companies is highly effective in providing intelligence to counter internal and external security threats. So the agencies required companies to retain data about their customers, available for access when there was a national security or policing need.

Thanks to the revelations of an ex-CIA contractor, Edward Snowden, we have a better understanding of how much our government had secretly monitored our data. In 2013, he leaked around 1.7 million classified documents to journalists. They revealed the NSA's online espionage and its global surveillance programmes in partnership with other countries in the 'five eyes' – Australia, Canada, New Zealand and the UK. They revealed that the British intelligence and security organisation, GCHQ, was siphoning our private data from businesses, including Microsoft, Google, Facebook and Apple. It was also undermining the technology that was meant to make the internet secure.

Snowden brought to light a programme suggesting that GCHQ had set up a system, called Tempora, for storing all internet traffic entering and leaving the United Kingdom. An estimated ten to twenty-five per cent of global internet traffic travels through the UK via underwater fibre optic cables.[33] The Home Office and the agencies have neither confirmed nor denied Tempora's existence – but claim that they must collect

---

32 Glenn Greenwald, *No Place to Hide: Edward Snowden, the NSA and the Surveillance State* (London: Penguin, 2015) and 'Why Privacy Matters', *TED Talk*, October 2014 (online video).
33 David Anderson QC, *A Question of Trust: Report of the Investigatory Powers Review,* June 2015, Chapter 4, §4.13.

digital data in bulk so they can target particular persons of interest. That is an enormous shift from the way that surveillance used to happen, with consequences for the relationship between citizen and state. Instead of identifying specific people who pose a threat and then putting them under surveillance, the idea is to put everyone under surveillance and decide later who poses a threat.

Surveillance powers are indispensable to the work of the police and security services and necessarily sweepingly broad. Criminals and terrorists use technology to plot and execute their crimes. Their communications must be closely monitored if their plans are to be frustrated. Packages containing contraband must be intercepted before they arrive in the country. DNA evidence is vital to solving heinous crimes. Bodily searches thwart drug smugglers.

So how much of our private lives should we sacrifice to keep ourselves safe and our borders secure? Most of us do not object to the use of CCTV in public places, though its overuse makes us uneasy. We accept that (with a warrant based on reasonable grounds) police can enter and search our homes. We are less happy when agents of the state spy on our telephone conversations, emails and text messages. On the other hand, how else can we be protected against the devastating effects of cyber warfare – arguably a greater threat these days than nuclear warfare?

Surveillance must be secret if it is to be effective. Yet secrecy makes it impossible to know and ensure that public authorities do not stray beyond their powers. In the absence of effective public scrutiny, there is a pressing need for strong legal safeguards against abuse. Yet such safeguards have not kept pace with technological change. The speed of the digital revolution made it difficult to maintain a fair balance between secrecy and openness. Britain tilts too far towards a closed society. Through excessive secrecy and opposition to much-needed reforms, the security and intelligence agencies and their political masters have sapped public confidence in their vital work.

Big Brother

The tradition of secrecy was strengthened during the Second World War to protect the vital work done at Bletchley Park by code breakers led by Alan Turing and Gordon Welchman.[34] The agencies operated in the dark until the end of the 1980s. The policy of successive governments was to refuse to disclose any information about what they were doing. The basis for their powers was not in enacted law but in a Home Office directive published in September 1952, at the height of the Cold War. It listed 'defence of the realm' as the object of their work and appointed a Director General responsible for making sure they did not stray beyond what was 'strictly . . . necessary for the purposes of the task'.

The directive specified that no work was to be done without an important public interest, no work targeting a particular section of the community and that the service must be free from political bias. But the directive had no legal force. No court or parliamentary watchdog committee could scrutinise whether the agencies kept faith with these orders. Parliament was not involved and even ministers were kept in the dark.

In 1976, Home Secretary Roy Jenkins set up a Committee on Data Protection chaired by Sir Norman Lindop. It was to

---

34 Gordon Welchman, *The Hut Six Story: Breaking the Enigma Codes* (New York: McGraw-Hill, 1982). Welchman lost his job as a result of publishing his story.

examine how to protect personal data in light of the advent of personal computers – but the Committee was refused access to information about the security services' systems 'in the interests of national security'. Lindop commented that secrecy, while necessary to intelligence work, left the agencies:

> In a hermetic compartment where they can never discuss their problems with anyone outside their own tight community; thus they are not open to the healthy – and often constructive – criticism and debate which assures for many other public servants that they will not stray beyond their allotted functions.[35]

The Lindop report called for powers to monitor the security services' compliance with a new data protection code. But Margaret Thatcher became Prime Minister six months later and the report was buried.

What was actually happening covertly came to light when Cathy Massiter, a former intelligence officer of MI5, blew the whistle in March 1985. It led Harriet Harman and Patricia Hewitt – future Labour Cabinet ministers – to complain to the Strasbourg Court of the violation of their right to privacy.

Harriet Harman was then a legal officer for the National Council for Civil Liberties (now known as Liberty) and Patricia Hewitt was General Secretary. The security service branded the NCCL a 'communist controlled subversive organisation' and Harman and Hewitt were placed in the category of 'communist sympathiser'. Spies intercepted the mail and

---

35 Committee on Data Protection, *Data Protection: Committee Report*, Cmnd 7341, 1978, §23.21.

phone calls of some of their clients. Whenever those clients made reference to either Harman or Hewitt, a member of the Security Service recorded it. The records were put into files to assess the 'security fitness' of the two women when they became parliamentary candidates.[36]

In 1992, the European Commission of Human Rights found that the government had acted unlawfully when it restricted Harman and Hewitt's right to privacy – because its power to put them under surveillance was not based on a clear or accessible legal framework.[37] Wisely, the government did not attempt to challenge these findings in the Strasbourg Court. Instead, it introduced a law to place the work of the security services on a statutory footing – for the first time ever.[38] It also established the first Security Service Commissioner and a Tribunal to investigate complaints about the service. In 1994, Parliament set up the Intelligence and Security Committee, the first Committee to provide a measure of democratic oversight.

It was a victory for transparency and the rule of law, but it did not end the abuses. The Strasbourg Court found the UK in breach in 1997, for intercepting police internal communications;[39] again, in 2000, in relation to other covert listening devices;[40] and yet again, in 2002, for intercepting messages to pagers over a private

---

36 It was standard practice to provide the Cabinet Office with assessments of newly elected MPs where the security and intelligence agencies found cause for concern about their 'security fitness' to take part in parliamentary committees with access to classified information.

37 *Harman and Hewitt v United Kingdom* (1992) 14 EHRR 657.

38 The Security Services Act 1989. The Intelligence Services and Security Service Acts followed in 1994 and 1996. In 1997, Parliament enacted Part III of the Police Act in response to adverse rulings in Strasbourg.

39 *Halford v UK* (1997) 24 EHRR 523.

40 *Khan v UK* (2000) 31 EHRR 1016.

network.[41] The Home Office introduced piecemeal measures in grudging responses to these judgments. But it was not until the coming into force of the Human Rights Act in 2000 that Parliament passed a consolidated law to regulate electronic surveillance – the Regulation of Investigatory Powers Act (RIPA).

RIPA governs the interception of electronic communications as they are being transmitted, such as the contents of emails. The agencies, the Ministry of Defence, selected police forces and the Inland Revenue may intercept electronic data if they obtain a warrant authorised by a relevant minister.[42] Ministers must be satisfied the interception is necessary on grounds of national security, preventing or detecting serious crime, safeguarding the economic well-being of the UK or for the purpose of giving effect to an international agreement – *and* that the interference with privacy is proportionate to that need.[43] But ministers are neither independent nor impartial. The public would trust judges rather than politicians to maintain the right balance between security and liberty. That is the position in the USA, Canada, Australia and New Zealand.[44]

RIPA also created another set of less restricted powers to collect what is called 'communications data'. This refers to data *about* a communication but not its contents. Communications data reveals the identity of those using internet and mobile services, where we are when they use them, whom we contact,

---

41 *Taylor-Sabori v UK* (2003) 36 EHRR 248.
42 The Home Secretary, Foreign Secretary, Northern Ireland Secretary or Scottish Ministers.
43 Section 5(3) Regulation of Investigatory Powers Act 2000.
44 An Interception of Communications Commissioner oversees the operation of warrants through a team of inspectors reporting biannually. However, he reviews only a small sample of all warrants authorised and does so retrospectively.

when, how often and for how long. It includes information we give to websites and providers when we sign up – names, addresses, phone numbers, bank account data.

About six hundred different public authorities can access communications data from service providers (as opposed to just nine that can intercept a communication's contents).[45] Yet surveillance of communications data can be more intrusive than reading emails or text messages: with enough of it, it is easy to model the entirety of a person's most important movements, activities, interests and relationships. We keep our smartphones with us around the clock and with them the GPS technology that tracks our location. We leave digital footprints whenever we make a call, write an email, send a text, pay with our bank cards, search the internet, use social media, save our files online, walk past a security camera, enter the sightline of anyone taking a photo, or do just about anything else.

Despite this, warrants for intercepting communications data do not need to be signed off by ministers. People *within* the organisation seeking the data may do so – usually middle management, such as a superintendent within a police force.

RIPA is now fifteen years old. It has been amended (but not replaced) in patchwork fashion by other parallel and piecemeal statutes. The mass of communications data available today was not envisaged when it was enacted. It has been interpreted to cover forms of technology that did not exist when it was passed. At that time, only a quarter of UK homes were connected to the internet and only half of adults had mobile phones.[46] There was

---

45 The list is set out in RIPA Part 1 Chapter 2.
46 David Anderson QC, *A Question of Trust: Report of the Investigatory Powers Review,* June 2015, Chapter 4, §4.6.

no Facebook, no Twitter, no Skype – and Google was still being run out of a garage.

The United States authorities welcomed the United Kingdom's surveillance cooperation because – as one leaked memo suggested – our country enjoys 'a more permissive legal environment'. When Snowden's allegations came to light, the US Congress responded by passing a Freedom Act in 2015, curtailing the ability of the US government and its agents to engage in bulk collection of citizens' data. There has been no comparable legislation in the UK. A key parliamentary report even gave the agencies' bulk interception capabilities a clean bill of health.[47]

Part of the problem has been weak parliamentary oversight of the agencies' work. Only the Intelligence and Security Committee is permitted to conduct parliamentary scrutiny. But the Prime Minister has an absolute veto over the Committee's membership, the evidence it can examine and what information it can make public. The Committee did not report on GCHQ's bulk surveillance programmes until the Snowden revelations brought them to light. In July 2014, it issued a statement about allegations that GCHQ had circumvented the law, describing them as unfounded.[48]

That was also the month that the government decided to rush emergency legislation through Parliament to give it continued access to communications data held by internet and telecoms companies. After Snowden had exposed their cooperation with

---

47 Intelligence and Security Committee, *Privacy and Security: A Modern and Transparent Legal Framework*, 12 March 2015, HC Paper 1075.
48 Intelligence and Security Committee, *Statement on GCHQ's Alleged Interception of Communications under the US PRISM Programme*, 17 July 2013, p. 2.

governments, Google, Facebook, Microsoft, LinkedIn and Yahoo started taking a more customer-oriented stance to privacy. They developed better encryption technology for many of their services. They committed to defending the rights of users when confronted with government demands that break international law and standards. Many signed up to the Reform Government Surveillance Coalition, which advocates that governments should limit surveillance to specific users for lawful purposes. Some produced annual transparency reports, which provide broad data about government information requests they receive.

The government's legal basis for requiring companies to hand over their data was not a domestic statute but a European directive. In April 2014, the European Court of Justice declared that directive invalid, because it violated the rights to privacy and data protection under the EU Charter of Fundamental Rights.[49] The coalition government feared that the ruling would lead companies to destroy their records. So three months later it used an emergency procedure to hasten a new law through Parliament.[50] The law's stated purpose was to ensure there was a temporary legal basis for what the authorities were already doing. But the Luxembourg Court's ruling had raised questions about whether what they did *ever* had a lawful basis.

Three months later, in October 2014, it emerged that police had been using RIPA to circumvent the law requiring judicial authorisation before seeking the identity of journalistic sources. That protection was in place for free expression – because many

---

49 *Digital Rights Ireland Ltd v Minister for Communications, Marine and Natural Resources* (Joined cases C293/12 and C594/12) [2015] QB 127.
50 The Data Retention and Investigatory Powers Act 2014.

people with information in the public interest would fail to come forward if they knew the authorities might be listening in. An independent inquiry concluded that over three years, nineteen police forces had made more than six hundred applications to uncover journalists' confidential sources.[51]

In November 2014, there were also press reports that RIPA had been used to circumvent the law protecting communications between lawyers and their clients.[52] Lawyers warned that dozens of terrorism-related cases over many years could have been tainted as a result. The Supreme Court had previously ruled that RIPA overrode the law protecting legal professional privilege and other rights of people in custody to confidential legal advice[53] – even though the issue was never debated in Parliament during the Act's passage. That is a slippery slope. Where fear of surveillance inhibits lawyer–client communication, the accuracy of legal advice is the casualty. It is not just individual privacy that is affected but the administration of justice as a whole.

It is manifestly unfair if one party to litigation has the power to monitor the confidential communications of the other. The government's position is that it can intercept lawyer–client communications without interfering with the right to a fair trial

---

51 Sir Anthony May, *IOCCO inquiry into the use of Chapter 2 of Part 1 of the Regulation of Investigatory Powers Act (RIPA) to identify journalistic sources*, 4 February 2015.
52 E.g. 'UK intelligence agencies spying on lawyers in sensitive security cases', *Guardian*, 7 November 2014; 'Revealed: spies eavesdrop on conversations with lawyers; MI5 and GCHQ allow interception despite material being legally protected', *Independent*, 7 November 2014; 'Spies eavesdropped on lawyers' conversations with their clients', *Times*, 7 November 2014.
53 *Re McE* [2009] UKHL 15.

– as long as police and intelligence agencies keep their work away from prosecutors. Yet abuses have already been well documented – as in 2011, when the Court of Appeal struck down the convictions of twenty environmental protestors for aggravated trespass because the prosecution had not been open about the role of an undercover police officer, Mark Kennedy.[54] Tasked with reporting on the proposed criminal activities of extreme left-wing protestors, Kennedy had infiltrated various campaigns. He was present when protestors received legal advice about the risks associated with their plan to occupy a power station.

Public outcry at what had been happening in secret eventually mobilised the political classes. Having enacted emergency law, the authorities responded to the new mood by publicly attacking internet and telecoms companies for changing their stance. GCHQ's Director alleged in November 2014 that search engines had effectively become 'command-and-control networks for terrorists and criminals'. He complained they were in denial about their role and not doing enough to facilitate lawful investigations.[55] David Cameron accused them of allowing their networks to be used 'to plot murder and mayhem' and demanded they live up to their social responsibilities.[56] Neither the Director nor the Prime Minister, however, acknowledged the government's involvement in undermining customer trust and ultimately provoking the private sector's response.[57]

---

54 *R v Barkshire* [2011] EWCA Crim 1885.
55 Robert Hannigan, 'The web is a terrorist's command-and-control network of choice', *Financial Times*, 3 November 2014.
56 'Lee Rigby: internet firms providing safe haven for terrorists, says PM', *Guardian*, 25 November 2015.
57 'Facebook was no more culpable in Lee Rigby's murder than MI5. David Cameron should not use it as a scapegoat', *Times*, 27 November 2014.

The Commons Home Affairs Committee conducted an inquiry into police officers' use of communications data under RIPA. In December 2014, it published a report concluding that the legal regime was not fit for purpose.[58] The Committee said there was a complete lack of public disclosure, lamented the extensive powers given to ministers and described the way the agencies recorded information as 'secretive, disorganised and totally insufficient'. Police officers in many cases did not know the professions of individuals whose data they were requesting. There was no requirement to record it, even if the data was taken from lawyers or journalists.

The Strasbourg Court has set out the minimum standards that apply under the Convention. The authorities must be transparent about the circumstances under which we face surveillance and the legal safeguards against abuse of those powers. The law must limit the duration of interception, set out the procedure for examining and storing data, contain precautions about communicating it to third parties and make clear the circumstances in which it must be destroyed.[59]

These standards need to be applied by our courts. But there are well-founded criticisms of the weakness of judicial as well as parliamentary oversight. RIPA created a special Investigatory Powers Tribunal (IPT), the only judicial body in the UK with the power to investigate the agencies. Initially hearings were held in private and judgments rarely made public. There was no way to appeal them except by taking a case to the European

58 HC Home Affairs Committee, *Regulation of Investigatory Powers Act 2000*, HC Paper 711, 3 December 2014.
59 *Weber and Saravia v Germany* (2008) 46 EHRR SE5, §93–95 (admissibility decision). See also *Malone v UK* (1985) 7 EHRR 14; *Khan v UK* (2000) 31 EHRR 1016; *Liberty v UK* (2009) 48 EHRR 1; *Kennedy v UK* (2011) 52 EHRR 4.

Court of Human Rights.[60] In its first thirteen years of operation, the IPT received more than 1,600 complaints. It upheld only ten – and five of them were against members of the same family. None involved the agencies.

It was February 2015 before the IPT ruled against the agencies. It decided that some of the programmes revealed by Snowden breached the Convention – because the public did not have the minimum knowledge about what was happening needed to regulate their behaviour accordingly.[61] That was the same month that the government finally published a new Code of Practice for dealing with legally privileged communications – but still it lacked essential safeguards.[62]

Yet the tide was turning in favour of change. The Intelligence and Security Committee conducted an inquiry and, in March 2015, it reported that the legal framework governing access to private communications was inadequate in the internet age.[63] Parliament also approved changes to the

---

60 The Strasbourg Court is expected soon to rule on whether the UK regime satisfies the Convention: *Big Brother Watch & Ors v United Kingdom*, Joint Application No 58170/13 (ECHR, lodged on 4 September 2013).

61 *Liberty & Ors v GCHQ* [2015] 3 All ER 212. The intelligence agencies had refused to confirm or deny that the programmes leaked by Snowden were an accurate description of what they were doing, so the Tribunal proceeded on the basis of assumed facts.

62 To address the use of RIPA by police in uncovering journalists' sources, the government also amended the Communications Data Acquisition Code of Practice. It provided that applications to the court under the Police and Criminal Evidence Act 1984 be used until such a time as there is specific legislation to provide for judicial authorisation where communications data is sought to determine the source of journalistic information.

63 Intelligence and Security Committee, *Privacy and Security: A Modern Legal Framework*, 12 March 2015, HC Paper 1075.

Code of Practice governing public authorities' access to communications data, to give protection to communications between journalists and their sources.[64] Then in April 2015, the Investigatory Powers Tribunal ordered GCHQ to destroy illegally intercepted communications between a Libyan rendition victim, Abdel Belhadj, and his lawyer.[65] Belhadj is suing the UK government for alleged involvement in his rendition and torture, which made the breach of legal professional privilege particularly disquieting. In mishandling that data, GCHQ admitted it had broken its own rules and had broken the law.

Two months later, in June 2015, the government made public a review of the legal framework by the Independent Reviewer of Terrorism Legislation, David Anderson QC. He concluded that:

> RIPA, obscure since its inception, has been patched up so many times as to make it all but incomprehensible to a tiny band of initiates. A multitude of alternative powers, some of them without statutory safeguards, confuse the picture further. This state of affairs is undemocratic, unnecessary and in the long run, intolerable.[66]

---

64 No equivalent amendment was introduced to better protect legal or parliamentary privilege.
65 *Belhadj & Ors v Security Service & Ors* [2015] UKIP Trib 13_132–H. The decision was the first time the IPT has found in favour of an individual claimant, in an open judgment, and held that the agencies have acted unlawfully.
66 David Anderson QC, *A Question of Trust: Report of the Investigatory Powers Review,* June 2015, p. 8, §35.

Anderson emphasised that the road to a better system must be paved with trust – which depends not just on those in powerful institutions behaving themselves but on mechanisms to verify that they have done so.[67] He cautioned that:

> Such mechanisms are particularly challenging to achieve in the national security field, where potential conflicts between state power and civil liberties are acute, suspicion rife and yet information tightly rationed.

Shortly afterwards, the government accepted the need to replace RIPA.[68] The following month, the High Court ruled that the government's emergency legislation was incompatible with EU law – because like the earlier directive upon which it was based, it did not contain adequate safeguards against intrusion into privacy.[69]

Even with an overhaul of RIPA and stronger safeguards, however, there will remain the problem of effective oversight. The political wrangling will continue. The Intelligence and Security Committee made clear it believes that the power to sign off on interception warrants must be given to ministers rather than independent judges. David Anderson disagreed, as do I.

---

67 David Anderson QC, *A Question of Trust: Report of the Investigatory Powers Review,* June 2015, p. 246, §13.4.

68 HC Deb 11 June 2015, vol. 596, col. 1353. The Royal United Services Institute also published a report urging reform: *A Democratic Licence to Operate: Report of the Independent Surveillance Review,* July 2015.

69 *R (Davis et al) v Secretary of State for Home Department* [2015] EWHC 2092. The order to disapply the Data Retention and Investigatory Powers Act 2014 was suspended until March 2016, to enable Parliament to amend the law.

Ministers seek further powers to take remote control of electronic devices to access documents, photographs and communications inside them. They want to be free to break encryption technology that stands in the way of so doing. David Anderson has pointed out that such hacking activities had no 'clear and explicit basis in legislation'.[70]

I do not share the purist libertarian view that the state has no business snooping on the private affairs of the individual. Like Anderson, I accept that the agencies need wide powers of access to communications, including requiring service providers to retain and make available communications data relating to the whole population. However, firm limits must be written into our law – not merely safeguards, but red lines that may not be crossed.[71] The agencies seem aware that they must shift away from the attitude of the grumpy father in Ring Lardner's story.[72] His daughter asked tenderly, 'Are you lost, daddy?' 'Shut up,' he explained.

Life and death

The right to respect for private and family life encompasses not only complex policy choices involving surveillance in the digital age, but also matters of life and death. Among them are the right of patients to refuse life-saving medical treatment, or to terminate an unwanted pregnancy, and the rights and duties of doctors and nurses.

---

70 David Anderson QC, *A Question of Trust: Report of the Investigatory Powers Review,* June 2015, p. 214, §12.8.

71 David Anderson QC, *A Question of Trust: Report of the Investigatory Powers Review,* June 2015, p. 249, §13.18.

72 Ring Lardner, *The Young Immigrunts* (Indianapolis: Bobbs-Merrill, 1920).

These issues arose in cases in which I was professionally involved. Some would argue that judges should not decide them, but in the absence of action by Parliament, judges feel impelled to meet the justice of particular cases. The result is the haphazard and piecemeal judicial development of the law as it grapples with difficult ethical questions. What are the limits of a patient's right to choose whether to have medical treatment? Must we be allowed to make choices about what happens to our bodies whenever we have the capacity – even if the refusal of treatment would result in the worsening of our illness? What about when we no longer have the capacity – what then?

When he was seventeen years old, Anthony Bland was injured at the Hillsborough football ground. He sustained catastrophic and irreversible damage to his brain. He was permanently unconscious and kept alive by artificial feeding. His condition was horrific. He continued to breathe unaided and his digestion continued to function. But although his eyes were open, he could not see. He could not hear. He could feel no pain. He could not taste or smell. He could not speak or communicate in any way. He had no cognitive function and could feel no emotion, whether pleasure or distress. The space the brain should have occupied was full of watery fluid.

Anthony was technically alive but he had no life worth living. He was fed by mechanically pumping liquid food into a tube threaded down through his nose and into his stomach. His bowels were evacuated by enema and his bladder drained by catheter. He developed repeated urinary tract and chest infections. Informed and responsible medical opinion was that there was no hope of any improvement in his condition, although with skilled nursing and close medical attention he might continue to live this way for many years.

He could not choose whether to continue the medical treatment that kept him artificially alive, because he was permanently unconscious. Withdrawing medical support would allow Anthony to die peacefully and with dignity. His doctors feared that so doing might make them guilty of homicide, or breach of the ethics of their profession. The law was unclear on whether the sanctity of human life was absolute – even where the patient had not consented to medical treatment and it conferred no benefit on him.

The courts were asked to rule on the issue. I was instructed by the Attorney General to assist as *amicus curiae* (a friend of the court), free to argue as I saw fit. I am not a criminal lawyer nor a moral philosopher. Until I took part in the case, I had not thought much about the ethical issues it raised. But I knew that if the courts left the issue to Parliament, everyone would be kept in a state of uncertainty and Anthony would remain a passive prisoner of modern technology.

I argued that health professionals should not be obliged to strive officiously to keep Anthony Bland alive. Since he had no quality of life, withdrawal of artificial life support was in his best interests. The Law Lords agreed.[73] They ruled the profession had no duty to continue invasive care and treatment when the justification for it had gone. They also ruled that the court's approval should be sought before withdrawing medical treatment for any patient in a persistent vegetative state. That safeguard was in the interests of protecting patients and doctors, as well as reassuring patients' families and the public.

Two Law Lords, Browne-Wilkinson and Mustill, were troubled by what they had to decide. They believed it was imperative that Parliament rather than judges should resolve the moral,

---

73 *Airedale NHS Trust v Bland* [1993] AC 789 (HL).

social and legal issues. The advance of modern technology made this 'an ever more urgent task' because patients' lives are prolonged more now than ever before.[74]

Four years after Anthony's case, Annie Lindsell sought help. Annie was paralysed, suffering from motor neurone disease, a degenerative neurological condition with no known cause or cure. It kills the nerves controlling movement. Sufferers find themselves trapped inside a progressively paralysed body – but retain total brain function and are able to feel pain.

Annie wanted to remain at home until she died, rather than at a hospice. She wanted to be cared for by her loving friends, under the supervision of her doctor, consultant and the district nurse. She did not want invasive surgery, such as the insertion of a feeding tube. Nor did she want to live on in a doped haze. As her condition worsened she would become unable to swallow, at risk of choking to death. When the quality of her life became unacceptable, she wanted to be confident that her doctor could lawfully treat her with a high dose of morphine, to enable her to die peacefully. The drug would relieve her severe distress, even though it would shorten her life.

Annie also hoped that her case would help result in law reform for those in her terrible condition. Before the Family Court we argued that doctors should have a defence to murder under three specific conditions: (i) the patient is dying; (ii) the patient finds life intolerable; and (iii) the only possible humane treatment has death as its consequence. We made clear that the defence should apply only if the patient had given informed and recent consent; and only if the treatment is administered in good faith, in accordance with good medical practice.

---

74 *Airedale NHS Trust v Bland* [1993] AC 789 (HL), *per* Lord Mustill, at §891A–C.

All the doctors and lawyers involved in our application to the court agreed that what was proposed was lawful. However, the judge made it plain that he was reluctant to rule on the issue. The prospect of appeals giving rise to delay and expense led us to withdraw the case. Annie died of pneumonia and the law remained uncertain.

Other patients tried to persuade the courts to decide that assisting terminally ill patients to commit suicide was not a crime. Like Annie, Diane Pretty suffered from motor neurone disease. The Director of Public Prosecutions refused to say whether her husband would be prosecuted for helping her commit suicide. In 2002, she took her case to the European Court of Human Rights. It made clear that the right to privacy involves a right to make decisions about our bodies and what happens to them, including choices about how to end our lives. But that right had to be balanced against the need to protect vulnerable people. Weighing the risk of abuse and relaxing the prohibition on assisted suicide were matters for national authorities. So the law, again, could not help.

Debbie Purdy suffered from progressive multiple sclerosis, a disease of the brain and spinal cord. She wanted to end her life at a point when it became unbearable – but she would then be too weak to do so without assistance. Her husband was willing to help but it was unclear whether he might be prosecuted under section 2(1) of the Suicide Act 1961. Debbie Purdy sought clarification from the authorities. When they refused, she won a victory at the House of Lords. The Law Lords ruled that the Director of Public Prosecutions should publish a policy identifying the factors underlying a decision to bring a prosecution for assisted suicide.[75]

---

75 The Director of Public Prosecutions did so: The Crown Prosecution Service, *Policy for Prosecutors in Respect of Cases of Encouraging or Assisting Suicide,* February 2010.

Lacking sufficient reassurances that her husband would not be prosecuted, Debbie chose not to go to Switzerland, where assisted suicide is legal. Debbie died in December 2014, having starved herself to death.

In that year, the Supreme Court heard another appeal, from Tony Nicklinson, who had suffered a catastrophic stroke when he was fifty-one. He was not terminally ill but totally paralysed, able to move only his head and eyes. He could communicate only by blinking to spell out words, letter by letter, using a computer. Tony Nicklinson described his life as dull, miserable, demeaning, undignified and intolerable; he wished to end it. But without assistance from a doctor, his only option was self-starvation – long, painful and drawn-out.

The Supreme Court, by a majority, dismissed his appeal. It could have ruled on whether the ban against assisted suicide was compatible with the Convention right to privacy. Instead, the Supreme Court decided to give Parliament another opportunity to consider the issue.[76]

There have been repeated attempts to persuade Parliament to permit doctor-assisted suicide. Lord Joffe introduced four Private Members' Bills. His last Bill, in 2006, was modelled on law which had worked successfully for eight years in the US state of Oregon. It applied only to patients with terminal illnesses, and only while they were able to administer the fatal drug themselves. It would not have assisted anyone in Mr Nicklinson's situation. The House of Lords blocked the Bill in May 2006.

---

76 R (on the application of Nicklinson) v Ministry of Justice [2014] UKSC 38. Two Justices in the minority (Lady Hale and Lord Kerr) would have issued a declaration of incompatibility.

In 2013, Lord Falconer introduced another Bill allowing doctor-assisted suicide for terminally ill patients with less than six months to live. It was narrowly confined and contained detailed safeguards against abuse. The patients had to be terminally ill. No one could be given a prescription unless they had the mental capacity to request it. Then they had to make a declaration as to their voluntary, clear and settled wish, signed by a witness and countersigned by two independent doctors. Once they were given the prescription, they could revoke the declaration if they changed their mind at any future point. The House of Lords introduced yet another safeguard, requiring judges to approve all applications for assisted death. The Bill was minimalist – leaving out patients in unendurable pain and distress with no end in sight. It died before the 2015 General Election because the government would not give it sufficient parliamentary time.

At the start of the new 2015 Parliament, Rob Marris MP introduced a Bill that was almost identical. It contained such stringent safeguards that they were unlikely to benefit more than a tiny proportion of the terminally ill. Yet the Archbishop of Canterbury, Lord Welby, urged MPs to reject it. He and the heads of other Christian, Jewish, Muslim and Sikh groups believed it would lead to suicide being 'actively supported' instead of viewed as a tragedy – and that would put thousands of vulnerable people at risk.[77]

Not all religious leaders agree with the position taken by the Church of England. The former Archbishop of Canterbury Lord Carey supports assisted dying legislation. So does Rabbi

---

77 Justin Welby, 'Why I believe assisting people to die would dehumanise our society for ever', *Guardian*, 5 September 2015.

Dr Jonathan Romain, who heads the group Inter-faith leaders for Dignity in Dying, numbering some fifty leaders of many religious affiliations. Rabbi Romain argues that assisted dying for the terminally ill who are mentally competent and request it of their own free will is not a mortal sin but a religious option.

On 11 September 2015, against the tide of public opinion, the House of Commons overwhelmingly rejected the Bill. As a result, the courts will be reluctant to intervene during the life-time of this Parliament.

Privacy and abortion

Just as doctor-assisted suicide for the terminally ill raises profound ethical issues, the conflict between pro-choice and pro-life raises difficult ethical dilemmas for doctors, social workers, lawyers and judges.

The European Court of Human Rights has made clear that anti-abortion laws and other regulations on the interruption of pregnancy interfere with a pregnant woman's right to privacy. But whenever a woman is pregnant, her private life becomes closely connected with the developing foetus. Member states vary in their stance towards abortion, so there are limited circumstances in which it is legitimate for the Court to rule on the issue.[78]

Abortion is permitted in most European countries to save the mother's life, preserve her mental and physical health, or in cases where pregnancy results from rape or incest. In most

---

78 They include where pregnancy and delivery pose a risk to the mother's health: *Tysiac v Poland* (2007) 45 EHRR 42, §106; *A, B and C v Ireland* (2011) 53 EHRR 13.

European countries an abortion can usually be carried out at the request of the mother, up to a certain stage in the development of the foetus – during the first twenty-four weeks in England, Scotland and Wales.[79]

In Northern Ireland, objection to abortion is deep-rooted. Abortion is a crime, carrying a maximum sentence of life imprisonment. The UK Parliament's Abortion Act 1967 does not apply there and the Northern Irish authorities are implacably opposed to its extension. Anyone who knows about an abortion and fails to pass information to the authorities risks ten years in prison.[80] There are exceptions where the mother's life is at risk, or she faces permanent and serious damage to her mental health. But their scope is unclear.[81] The UN Committee on the Elimination of Discrimination Against Women and the Committee on Economic, Social and Cultural Rights have both urged reform of Northern Irish abortion law in vain.[82]

---

79 In rarer situations, the law permits that abortion may be carried out after twenty-four weeks, if it is necessary to (i) save the woman's life, (ii) prevent grave permanent injury to the physical or mental health of the pregnant woman, or (iii) if there is substantial risk that the child would be born with serious physical or mental disabilities.

80 Section 5 Criminal Law Act (Northern Ireland) 1967.

81 Sections 58–59 Offences Against the Person Act 1861; sections 25–26 Criminal Justice Act (Northern Ireland) 1945. An offence under section 58 is punishable with imprisonment for life or for any shorter term.

82 UN Committee on the Elimination of Discrimination Against Women (CEDAW), *Concluding observations of the Committee on the Elimination of Discrimination against Women*, CEDAW/C/UK/CO/6, 10 July 2008, §289; CEDAW, *Concluding observations on the seventh periodic report of the United Kingdom of Great Britain and Northern Ireland*, CEDAW/C/GBR/CO/7, 30 July 2013, §50–51; *Concluding observations*

Facing an uncertain risk of prosecution, many pregnant women seeking terminations travel to mainland Britain (if they can afford it). Some eight hundred abortions a year are carried out in England and Wales for women who reside in Northern Ireland (exact figures are impossible to come by, as some women give false addresses for fear of detection). They suffer inevitable delay, which increases their stress, worsens the risk of psychological harm and bars them from accessing earlier, less invasive termination procedures. Their stress and harm is exacerbated by limited access to vital post-abortion medical care and counselling on their return home. Other women who cannot afford to travel take the risk of unsafe illegal backstreet terminations, endangering their health and even their lives.

Uncertainty also deters healthcare professionals from performing abortions and from giving advice to pregnant women. One notorious 1993 case involved a pregnant fourteen year-old in a children's home. She had threatened suicide if she was refused an abortion and repeatedly punched herself in the stomach to induce a miscarriage. The High Court decided that in those circumstances, a doctor who terminated her pregnancy in good faith would not face prosecution. But no doctor could be found in Northern Ireland willing to perform the operation. She had to travel to Liverpool.[83]

The Family Planning Association of Northern Ireland (FPANI) is the only pregnancy advisory service to have survived intimidation by anti-abortion campaigners. It gives counselling, information and support to women faced with unwanted

---

of the Committee on Economic, Social and Cultural Rights, E/C.12/GBR/CO/5, 12 June 2009, §25.
83 *Northern Health and Social Services Board v F and G* [1993] NI 268.

pregnancies. In 2003, FPANI instructed me to seek judicial review of the government's failure to clarify abortion law. The Northern Ireland executive has a statutory duty to give guidance to healthcare professionals and pregnant women about what is and is not lawful – including how women can have access to safe abortions.

The High Court allowed religious and pro-life organisations to make submissions to the Court. Their counsel gave biblical readings in support of their opposition to clarification of the law. Outside a group headed by a priest sang hymns and prayed against my legal team. I felt as though I was in a far-off country governed by a theocracy.

We lost in the High Court, but the Northern Ireland Court of Appeal ruled that official guidance was required.[84] The judgment was handed down in 2004 – but successive governments took another eight and a half years producing draft guidance for public consultation. While the executive stalled, pregnant women in Northern Ireland were denied protection of their rights.

In 2015, Northern Ireland's Human Rights Commission brought a new case to the High Court. It had repeatedly advised that prohibiting access to abortion violates the rights of women and girls in exceptional circumstances: when pregnancy results from rape or incest, or in cases involving serious malformation of the foetus. The government claimed that the law protected morals – but the judge noted that there was not 'one iota of evidence' that imposing criminal sanctions on women had resulted in the saving of pre-natal life. He pointed out that:

---

84 *Re Family Planning Association of Northern Ireland* [2003] NIQB 48; *Family Planning Association of Northern Ireland v Minister for Health, Social Services and Public Safety* [2004] NICA 39.

If it is morally wrong to abort a foetus in Northern Ireland, it is just as morally wrong to abort the same foetus in England. It does not protect morals to export the problem to another jurisdiction and then turn a blind eye.[85]

Though the situation cries out for reform, it is unclear whether the ruling will result in legislative change. Much depends on mustering political unity within the Northern Ireland Assembly. The impasse is unlikely to end soon.[86]

Reform is also important internationally. In 2012, an international NGO based in New York, the Global Justice Center, campaigned for humanitarian aid to enable safe abortions for victims of rape in armed conflict. In its most pernicious form, rape is used as a weapon of choice in the majority of today's armed conflicts, often with fatal consequences. About seventy per cent of conflict-related rapes in the Democratic Republic of Congo are gang rapes. Most are accompanied by mutilating injuries to women, including deliberate HIV infection. One-third of the victims of war rape in the DRC are under the age of eighteen. Many are raped in the context of sexual slavery. Many are routinely denied life- and health-saving abortions in humanitarian settings, leaving them with the terrible 'choices' of risking an unsafe abortion or bearing the child of their rapists.

Two powerful forces perpetuated this situation – the USA and the International Committee of the Red Cross (ICRC). The

---

85 *The Northern Ireland Human Rights Commission's Application* [2015] NIQB 96, §142.
86 At the time of writing, the Attorney General has stated his intention to appeal the judgment. The Health Minister, however, has circulated new draft guidelines in the aftermath of the ruling. They are yet to be made public. 'NI abortion law: Health Minister Simon Hamilton issues draft guidelines', *BBC News online*, 1 December 2015.

USA imposed a 'no abortion' ban on its foreign aid. It required all recipients to pledge not to use US funds to provide abortions. The ICRC's largest donor is the USA. Its operational guidelines forbade ICRC staff from performing abortions. The ICRC is the biggest recipient of UK government funds for humanitarian aid – so in effect, UK money was being segregated away from abortion services.

International humanitarian law permits foreign aid to be used for safe abortions – including in countries where national law forbids it. I initiated a debate in Parliament asking the coalition to clarify whether government-funded medical care included abortion services for war rape survivors. The government replied clearly and unequivocally that all UK-funded partners must abide by humanitarian principles. Given the partnership of the UK and the ICRC, this was in reality a new policy. It was followed up when the UK persuaded the UN Security Council to call for 'access to the full range of sexual and reproductive health services, including regarding pregnancies resulting from rape, without discrimination'. Soon after, the EU Commission also changed its stance to affirm that war rape victims have the right to receive all the medical care required by their condition, including abortion, irrespective of local laws in war zones.

What matters now

Brandeis and Warren declared in their seminal article on privacy that 'Political, social and economic changes entail the recognition of new rights, and the common law, in its eternal youth, grows to meet the new demands of society.'[87] Fine words but the situation is not so simple. Some of the issues are suitable to be

---

87 *Harvard Law Review*, vol. 4., No. 5, 1890, p. 193.

determined by unelected judges, but many are better determined by the elected legislature. In matters of law reform there is a constant tension between the judicial and political branches of government.

Judges have sometimes to decide whether to recognise new rights, such as the right to privacy, but they have to proceed with caution. They have no democratic mandate to make the law. Where Parliament fails to act, the courts try to do justice, if necessary relying on the broad principles protected by the common law and the Human Rights Act. I have not had that difficult task because I am not a judge. But as a lawmaker in government and Parliament I have had to make choices between using the common law and statute law in pursuing reforms.

Like the many committees that have looked at the problems of media intrusions on privacy, I do not think there is the need for further legislation on that subject. The Human Rights Act and the Convention work well in maintaining a balance based on the public interest. There is ample criminal law to tackle both the grossest forms of abuse and lesser wrongdoing. I believe in independent self-regulation not statutory regulation.

Despite the success of the celebrity-driven Hacked Off in campaigning for a punitive regime to govern the print media, I believe that the IPSO system, chaired by Sir Alan Moses, should be allowed to develop. That means that the press barons will have to accept his recommendations for procedural changes. I hope that the state-imposed regulatory scheme will be abolished by Parliament or declared unlawful by the Strasbourg Court.

The need for a new surveillance law is pressing. Though it is difficult for legislators to foresee the ways in which technology will advance, Parliament must address RIPA's obvious short-comings. A new communications data law, based on the recommendations of the Independent Reviewer of Terrorism Legislation, David Anderson, should give control of authorising interception to judges, not to ministers. It must contain safeguards to protect legal and journalistic privilege. It must give everyone a fair indication of the circumstances under which their data will be harvested. It must give the agencies the powers they need to keep our streets and borders safe – but subject to law and to proper limits. We also need stronger and better parliamentary oversight. Public trust and confidence are vital to the agencies' work.

Private companies have become better at safeguarding citizens' privacy against government intrusion. But they are less constrained when privacy invasion is in their commercial interests. If we wish to avoid a Balkanised internet, this is an issue that cannot be tackled by any one country unilaterally, or even at a regional level. It demands a cross-border approach, avoiding over-regulation.

Criminal law and medical law need to be amended to strengthen patient autonomy and choice. The old model of viewing patients as passive recipients of the informed paternalism of the medical profession is no longer appropriate. One day, Parliament will legalise doctor-assisted suicide, but it will not happen during this Parliament. Northern Ireland's abortion law needs reform, ending the pain and suffering endured by those who must travel to the mainland or else run the risks of a back-street abortion. And as regards war rape, the EU Commission has recently affirmed too that victims must have access to safe abortions. But as Janet Benshoof, the head of the Global Justice Center, wrote to me:

Words alone will not save the lives of girls and women impreg-
nated by rape. Getting the EU Commission to act aggressively
to ensure this policy is in place in every EU-funded facility in
every war zone, for every female victim of war rape, will not be
easy.

5

THE RULE OF LAW

'"The question is," said Alice, "whether you can make words mean
so many different things."
"The question is", said Humpty Dumpty, "which is to be master
– that's all".'
Lewis Carroll, *Through the Looking Glass* (1871)

'Supposing the invader wears not jackboots but carpet slippers or
patent leather pumps?'
Hubert Butler (ed. John Banville),
The Invader Wore Slippers (2012)

'The rule of law' is a weighty and ponderous phrase, much
quoted by politicians and judges but much misused, sometimes
risking becoming meaningless verbiage. It is under threat
everywhere.

To dictators the rule of law means blind obedience to the law
even if the law is arbitrary: a law is a law is a law. According to the
Nazi judges, the Nuremberg Decrees stripping German Jews of
their rights as citizens had to be obeyed because they were 'the

law'. The same was said of South Africa's apartheid laws and of the slave laws in the United States. That mindset is known as 'legal positivism' – a way of thinking that does not ask if the law is fair or reasonable but simply whether it is 'the law'.

Tom Bingham answered that way of thinking in his gem of a book on the rule of law:

> A state which savagely represses or persecutes sections of its people cannot in my view be regarded as observing the rule of law, even if the transport of the persecuted minority to the concentration camp or the compulsory exposure of female children on the mountainside is the subject of detailed laws duly enacted and scrupulously observed.[1]

Others argue that the law must be obeyed if and only if it has been made by a democratically elected legislature. That does not add much value because a democratically elected legislature may abuse its powers and violate the rule of law. Hitler's Third Reich was democratically elected.

Leaders of theocratic states – Muslim, Christian and Buddhist – insist that a law is not a law unless it accords with their beliefs. Their ideologies may be as much political as religious and may easily become a form of tyranny against those who do not share them – sanctioning the beheading of heretics, the burning of witches, capital punishment for blasphemy, or Jihadi murders.

When we say that a state is governed by the rule of law, we mean much more than that it has outward forms of legality. The Soviet Constitution proclaimed a wide array of civil, political, economic, social and cultural rights. But it gave no protection

---

1 Tom Bingham, *The Rule of Law* (London: Allen Lane, 2010), p. 67.

against the abuse of power in the name of the Motherland. It was rhetorical surplusage masking dictatorial oppression.

The rule of law cannot be upheld without an independent judiciary and legal profession. Without them, the state would be free to oppress society's unpopular minorities. The United States is a nation conceived with a profound commitment to liberty. Yet despite its constitutional commitment to due process of law, the President appoints federal judges on political grounds and state judges are elected after giving promises to decide cases in a particular way. That is not compatible with my idea of what the rule of law requires. Judges must be appointed on merit, not because of their views on controversial matters of the day or their support for a political party.

The rule of law is inherent in the European Convention on Human Rights. Yet the judges of the Strasbourg Court are nominated by governments and elected by politicians. A single judge of the Strasbourg Court may reject a case as 'inadmissible' without giving any reason or an opportunity for a claimant to reply.

The rule of law requires justice for all who seek it. That is impossible unless the poor and not-so-rich can enjoy effective access to the courts. The state must provide sufficient legal aid at public expense to those unable to afford it. It must not impose unreasonable fees on those who use the courts. Just as it must provide a comprehensive health service, so it must provide a comprehensive legal service. If the people the law is meant to protect cannot enforce their rights when needed, those rights are of no value.

Public confidence in the administration of justice depends on its openness, not what happened when a Roman emperor set out his commands at the top of pillars hidden from public gaze. All laws must be publicly proclaimed and accessible, so that people have a fair warning of the law's demands and can regulate their behaviour accordingly. Secret laws do not meet the demands of the rule of law.

Freedom of expression is essential for the rule of law to function. A free press must be able to report and criticise what is happening in the courts without risk of punishment. That does not mean trial by newspapers or television, which is why the media must be careful not to prejudice a jury's verdict in a criminal case. But it does mean that writers and journalists must be free to comment where there are grounds to believe that there has been a miscarriage of justice.

These values are rarely given effect, as I have learned from sometimes painful experience.

An inhuman decision

I have only ever argued one death penalty case. It was an appeal in 1980 from Singapore's courts to the Judicial Committee of the Privy Council, the most senior British judges sitting in London.[2] The right to appeal to the Privy Council had been accepted when Singapore became independent. It was heard by five Law Lords (although Lord Edmund-Davies dropped out before judgment after a fall) presided over by Lord Diplock, a judge whose intellect far exceeded his compassion. My client, Ong Ah Chuan, was one of several Singaporeans found guilty of trafficking in heroin. The death penalty was mandatory for the offence.

The Law Lords did not think it their role to question the decision of the authorities in Singapore, even though that was their constitutional duty. As I began my argument, Lord Diplock interrupted me.

---

2 *Ong Ah Chuan v Public Prosecutor* [1981] AC 648 (PC).

'Did you argue the constitutional issue in Singapore?' he asked.[3]

'No, My Lord.'

'In that case, you cannot argue it now,' he said.

'Then my client will stand condemned to die unheard,' I replied.

'Quite,' said Diplock.

Lord Scarman said gently that he would like to hear the argument.

'Clear the Bar,' Lord Diplock thundered.

Twenty minutes later we were readmitted, Scarman looking the worse for wear. Diplock told me that I could argue the case – as long as I did not cite the decisions of the US Supreme Court. Singapore's Constitution offered guarantees of liberty and equal protection of the law in the same terms as the American Bill of Rights. As Diplock must have known, the American decisions supported my argument that a mandatory death penalty was unconstitutional.

Singapore's Parliament had received medical evidence. It demonstrated that my client had possessed a relatively small amount of heroin – not enough to show he was dealing in the drug. Diplock refused to let me refer to that evidence even though it was in Singapore's parliamentary record. All my arguments were in vain. The Privy Council rejected the appeal and Ong and the other appellants were hanged.

Two decades later, Lord Bingham spoke in a very differently constituted Privy Council in another death penalty appeal.[4]

---

3 Appeals are allowed on specific points of law. As a general rule, lawyers cannot raise points that have not been argued in the lower courts in an appeal court.

4 *Reyes v The Queen* [2002] 2 AC 235 (PC), §45.

He declined to follow Ong's case, stating tactfully that human rights jurisprudence at the time had been 'rudimentary'. I wrote to Bingham expressing my delight and setting out what had happened in the case. He replied that he was shocked.

Singapore again

A few years after Ong's case, I had direct experience of the way justice was denied in Singapore. The case involved the founding father and Prime Minister of Singapore, Lee Kuan Yew, a charismatic politician widely admired across the world. He had studied law at Cambridge University in the late 1940s, at a time when the law gave wide latitude to state power at the expense of individual liberty. British courts were then more executive-minded and what we know as public law was undeveloped.

When Singapore attained self-government in 1959, its Constitution included a Bill of Rights guaranteeing liberty, equal protection of the law and free speech and association. However, the spirit and the letter of the Constitution were not upheld. Lee Kuan Yew enjoyed near-absolute power, with a huge parliamentary majority. He enacted laws controlling the media and stifling dissent. Singapore's judiciary allowed themselves to be used as puppets. And Lee Kuan Yew would not tolerate criticism of his regime. He deployed his powers to crush the opposition. He invented the authoritarian concept of 'Asian values' to refute human rights.

In May 1987, sixteen young people were arrested and held without trial in solitary confinement. Several were Catholics. The authorities alleged, ludicrously, that they were involved in a Marxist conspiracy to subvert the social and political system in

Singapore. A few weeks later, they arrested six more people. All were held under the Internal Security Act. British colonial rulers had found that Act very useful for eradicating Chinese secret societies, alleged communists and trade unionists. The new rulers found it useful to silence political dissent.

Teo Soh Lung was a young solicitor working with the Law Society of Singapore. She had written reports for the Law Society criticising the government's interferences with press freedom and the justice system. Lee Kuan Yew was incensed. He accused the Law Society of being involved in politics, even though reporting on Bills was one of its statutory functions. He set up a parliamentary select committee to investigate. The proceedings were televised, including Lee Kuan Yew's interrogation of Teo Soh Lung. She stood up to him and would not abandon her beliefs.

Teo Soh Lung was arrested, interrogated, detained for a few months and then released in 1987.[5] The following year, she and eight others issued a press statement denying the government's allegations and claiming they were victims of ill treatment. They were rearrested. Teo Soh Lung's lawyers were detained as well.

I met her in a cramped interview room in the detention centre. It had a filing cabinet in which we assumed there was a gadget eavesdropping on our conversation. She told me that her cell was full of mosquitoes. She had been interrogated for many hours in skimpy clothes in front of an air conditioner – but she had not been broken. Her family had been permitted to talk to her only through a glass screen. But she was more concerned with my well-being than her own.

---

5 Her account is in Teo Soh Lung, *Beyond the Blue Gate: Recollections of a Political Prisoner* (Singapore: Function 8 Limited, 2011).

We managed to improve the conditions under which she was being kept and the Singapore Court of Appeal ordered her release on the basis of a technicality. As she was leaving the detention centre she was rearrested and returned to solitary confinement.

Teo Soh Lung's only remaining hope was to appeal to the Privy Council. We knew that we could not succeed in challenging her detention in Singapore, but we were confident of victory in London. British judges were no longer timorous when marking the limits of state power.

The Singapore government knew that we intended to appeal to the Privy Council and must have realised that it was likely to lose. It hastily suspended the country's Bill of Rights and amended the Constitution to abolish the right to appeal to the Privy Council in pending and future constitutional cases. I gave a lecture at the School of Oriental and African Studies criticising what had happened in Singapore. A few days later, Singapore's chief immigration officer informed me that my permission to practise would be revoked. I was told that I would be allowed to bring only one final legal challenge in Singapore.

I went back, knowing that it was the last time I would meet Teo Soh Lung in captivity. I attempted to negotiate her release, in vain. I was followed everywhere and vilified by the Singapore press as I was flying back to London. Even before I had landed back in London, the British Foreign Secretary, Geoffrey Howe, had made a diplomatic protest about my treatment. Lord Alexander QC took my place as Teo Soh Lung's barrister. He argued brilliantly with no success. She remained in solitary confinement for a further eighteen months.

There may be a little more political freedom now in Singapore but it is still not a country governed by the rule of law.[6] The Singapore government is too successful in court against opposition politicians, parties, journalists and bloggers. Defamation law silences critics or drives them to bankruptcy. In 2014, a prominent blogger, Roy Ngerng Yi Ling, wrote a post alleging the Prime Minister had mismanaged Singapore's retirement savings system. The High Court found him guilty of defaming the Prime Minister.[7] In 2015, activist and blogger Alex Au was convicted of contempt of court for implying that the judiciary exhibited 'systemic bias' in constitutional challenges to the criminalisation of same-sex intercourse. He was fined 8,000 Singaporean dollars.[8]

Malaysia

The situation in Malaysia is also troubling. In 1988, I helped to organise an international judicial seminar series in Bangalore.[9] The series developed principles that were influential to judges across the Commonwealth, encouraging them to give a generous interpretation to their constitutional protections of human rights and the rule of law.

---

6 In 2015, Freedom House rated Singapore as a 'partly free' country with an overall score of 4 (out of the lowest possible score of 7). The country scored particularly badly for the rule of law (7 out of a highest possible score of 16). See also Human Rights Watch, *World Report 2014: Singapore* (USA: Human Rights Watch, 2013), pp. 381–84.

7 The Prime Minister's counsel has requested the Supreme Court make 'a very high award of damages' of up to $400,000. At the time of writing judgment had not yet been handed down.

8 Sex between men is criminalised in Singapore under section 377A of the country's penal code.

9 The first in a series of judicial conferences run by the NGO Interights (the International Centre for the Legal Protection of Human Rights) and the Commonwealth Secretariat between 1988 and 1998.

One participant was Tun Salleh Abas, head of the Malaysian judiciary. On his return home, he gave lectures about upholding the rule of law. They offended the Prime Minister, Dr Mahathir, and Tun Salleh Abas was removed from office. Five judges of Malaysia's Supreme Court defied the Prime Minister by seeking to rescind the suspension of their chief. They too were removed for alleged misconduct. A government-appointed Commission sat in judgment of them.

Tun Salleh Abas never returned to office. Two of the five Supreme Court judges were permanently removed. Twenty years later, a panel of eminent jurists chaired by the former Chief Justice of India, J.S. Verma, found their dismissal to have been unconstitutional. It called for immediate steps to 'redeem the people's faith in the credibility of the judiciary and the rule of law'.[10] There was no response and the rule of law in Malaysia has never fully recovered. In July 2015, newspapers reported that Najib Razak, the incumbent Prime Minister, had fired his Deputy and Attorney General in a Cabinet purge – to fend off claims that he had corruptly channelled US$700 million from a state-owned investment fund into his private account.[11]

Singapore and Malaysia are of course not the only countries where the rule of law has been undermined. Their significance is that they belong to the Commonwealth and are meant to share the principle of the rule of law as part of their common law heritage. The

---

10 *Report of the Panel of Eminent Persons to Review of 1988 Judicial Crisis,* 26 July 2008, p. 77, §24.2.1. The report was commissioned by the Malaysian Bar, LAWASIA, the International Bar Association's Human Rights Institute and Transparency International – Malaysia.
11 Richard Smart, 'Malaysian PM sacks Ministers in wide reshuffle', *Times,* 29 July 2015.

Hong Kong judiciary have shown the way in upholding the rule of law in spite of being subject to the People's Republic of China.

Threats to the rule of law in the UK

The rule of law has been gravely undermined in the UK. In the thirteenth century, Magna Carta famously declared that 'to no one will we sell, to no one will we deny right or justice'. Parliament in the Glorious Revolution held steadfast to the ideal that even the monarch must not be above the law. That remains true to this day. The courts are now willing to review prerogative powers if they are abused.[12]

Our judges are independent and impartial. They do their best to uphold the rule of law against encroachments by the political branches of government, but there is no equality of arms between the judges and a government able to command a majority in Parliament.

No law and no system of government can secure the rule of law unless it is supported by a culture of respect for the rule of law and unless men and women of integrity hold it in their DNA. But the system of government can help or hinder respect for the rule of law. Our system is in urgent need of repair.

Unlike the rest of Europe and most of the common law world, we do not have a written constitution protecting fundamental rights and freedoms. Unlike most modern democracies, our system of government does not fully separate the three branches

---

12 These are historical powers officially held by the monarchy that are now exercised by the government on the Queen's behalf. Prerogative powers include declaring war, dispensing honours, appointing and dismissing ministers, assenting to international treaties, dissolving Parliament and calling elections.

of the state. Ministers are Members of Parliament as well as the executive and, until the birth of the Supreme Court of the United Kingdom in 2009, our senior judges sat as members of the House of Lords and could take part in political debates.

Before the Constitutional Reform Act 2005, the Lord Chancellor was at the heart of government, bringing together the executive, Parliament and the judiciary. He (no woman ever held the office) was head of the judiciary and able to sit as a judge – but also a senior politician and a Cabinet Minister, with responsibility for ensuring that the rule of law was respected within government. It was a bewildering combination of roles requiring the Lord Chancellor to be a contortionist. It became increasingly difficult to justify a system in which the chief judge in the final Court of Appeal was also a Cabinet Minister – especially as the Law Lords dealt with issues about the government's conduct.

That situation began to change in 2003. There was a drama reminiscent of a Shakespearean tragedy. It involved the fall of a man of high estate – Tony Blair's Lord Chancellor and former pupil-master at the Bar, Derry Irvine of Lairg. After portraying himself as a latter-day Cardinal Wolsey, he became a target of press ridicule. Political cartoonists drew him wearing a cardinal's vestments. He was accused in the press of improvidence and unnecessary luxury. It was even claimed that he had ordered his staff to peel his oranges to avoid getting himself sticky.

Much of this was unfair. Derry Irvine had his eccentricities but he had played a key role in New Labour's constitutional reforms, including the making of the Human Rights Act. He had also defended the rule of law and human rights courageously – refusing, for example, to allow newspapers to be exempt from liability for unwarranted intrusions on the private lives of celebrities.

Like Wolsey, he incurred his political master's displeasure and was summarily dismissed. Tony Blair replaced him with his good friend Charlie Falconer, a distinguished former member of the commercial Bar. The Prime Minister at first wanted to abolish the ancient office of Lord Chancellor. When Blair realised that technicalities would make abolition difficult, he abandoned the attempt. Instead he appointed Falconer as Secretary of State for Constitutional Affairs while also retaining the title of Lord Chancellor.

It was a hurried and botched reform that meant that a politician could be both a politically active heavyweight and a Lord Chancellor with a duty to protect the rule of law. It opened the way to later inroads on the rule of law.

The Constitutional Reform Act 2005 also brought in much-needed change. It took away ministers' ability to appoint senior judges on political grounds. Instead, the Act created an independent Judicial Appointments Commission and an independent Supreme Court. It also reformed the role of Lord Chancellor. He retained responsibility for the Ministry of Justice but was no longer permitted to head the judiciary.[13] Parliament envisaged that in addition to being departmental Minister of Justice, the Lord Chancellor would have special responsibility for upholding the rule of law. He would protect the independence of the justice system by securing proper resources for it; and he would protect the independence of judges by ensuring their freedom from political pressure.

The Act also made it possible for the Lord Chancellor to be an active serving politician with no legal qualifications or

---

13 That position is now held by the Lord Chief Justice of England and Wales, the highest judge of the courts of England and Wales. The Lord Chief Justice is also President of the Criminal Division of the Court of Appeal.

experience, rather than a distinguished jurist with a lifetime's experience in legal practice. By his oath of office, the new Lord Chancellor swore to defend the independence of the judiciary. When the Act was passed it was agreed that the oath imposed a higher duty than political advantage. But the Lord Chancellor was no longer a detached figure in government. In 2012, Chris Grayling MP became the first Lord Chancellor in modern times with no legal qualifications or experience. The rule of law was not part of his DNA, as he showed in a series of ill-begotten measures.

The House of Lords Constitution Committee made recommendations to strengthen the Lord Chancellor's duty in relation to the rule of law. Chris Grayling rejected all of them.[14] He and his ministerial colleagues also rejected the recommendation that the Lord Chancellor should have oversight of the constitution as a whole, to ensure the overall coherence of reforms made by other departments. That oversight is particularly important because of the need for an enduring constitutional framework for a stable union of nations across the UK.

Access to justice

Chris Grayling introduced measures that obstructed access to justice. First were political attacks on legal aid that are not likely to be reversed in the current political climate. In 1949, even amidst stringent post-war austerity, the Attlee government

---

14 House of Lords Constitution Committee, *The Office of Lord Chancellor*, 11 December 2014, Sixth Report of Session 2014–15, HL Paper 75; HL Deb 7 July 2015, vol. 764, cols. 104–139. I am a member of the Constitution Committee.

introduced the Legal Aid and Advice Act. The idea was that no one should be unable to defend a legal right or bring a just and reasonable claim because of cost.

Those accused of a crime were given help in defending themselves; as was anyone threatened with loss of livelihood. Parents fighting custody battles were given assistance so that the outcome reflected the best interests of their children and not the interests of whichever parent was better positioned to afford a lawyer. When in 1981 there were documented instances of assault and intimidation at police stations, legal aid was extended to suspects questioned over a crime. Those who claimed to be fleeing from persecution also received assistance in lodging an application for asylum.

Successive governments began to chip legal aid to the bone. In 1949, eight in ten people had access to legal aid based on income and assets. By 1986, six in ten were eligible. In 1999, the Access to Justice Act took away aid for people who suffered injuries as a result of negligence. It was claimed, dubiously, that the measures would not inhibit access to justice because lawyers would take cases on a 'no win, no fee' basis. By 2008, just shy of three in ten people satisfied the means test.

In 2009, an independent review concluded that it would be wrong to tighten the criteria for legal aid any further.[15] But the coalition government decided that it still cost too much. It introduced legislation sweeping whole areas of law out of the safety net: family, debt, housing, employment, immigration, medical negligence, education and welfare benefits – with narrow

---

15 Lord Justice Jackson, *Review of Civil Litigation Costs: Final Report*, January 2010, Chapter 7, p. 70, §4.2.

exceptions.[16] The House of Lords voted against the legislation fourteen times before it squeaked through.

The yearly budget for civil legal aid before those cuts was £2 billion in total – equivalent to running the NHS for a fortnight and less than a quarter of the cost of the 2012 London Olympics. The legislation sought to reduce it by £350 million.[17] In the year it took effect, the coalition announced plans to cut criminal legal aid as well, reducing the legal aid budget by £220 million every year until 2018. Barristers went on strike for the first time in recorded history.

Inevitably, courts have become less efficient, costing the taxpayer money. Without legal advice, cases that could be settled now go to trial, prolonging the parties' stress and putting further strain on the court system.[18] There have been outbreaks of courtroom violence. Complex fraud trials have been abandoned because no barrister could be found to represent the defendant at the price offered by the Legal Aid Agency. Legal advice centres have shut down. Litigants are forced to represent themselves.

---

16 Legal Aid, Sentencing and Punishment of Offenders Act 2012. The government envisaged only narrow exceptions involving the most vulnerable litigants – such as where family cases involve domestic violence, forced marriage or the risk of children being taken into care, or an appeal against welfare benefits involves the risk of losing a home.

17 In the year it took effect, expenditure on civil legal aid was reduced by £141 million. Expenditure on civil legal aid went from £942 million in 2012–13 to £801 million in 2013–14. House of Commons Public Accounts Committee, *Implementing Reforms to Civil Legal Aid,* 19 January 2015, Thirty-sixth Report of Session 2014–15, HC Paper 808, p. 4.

18 Mediations for family law matters fell by 38% in the year after the reforms, rather than increasing by 74% as the Ministry expected. *Implementing Reforms to Civil Legal Aid,* p. 4, §2.

Court time is wasted.[19] The victims of the cuts are society's vulnerable at crisis points in their lives: people with physical and mental disabilities, those with no means to support themselves other than from state benefits, the children of parents in custody battles, the victims of unscrupulous employers.

The cuts came at a time of stringent reductions to other public services, when the need for access to justice is even greater. When people cannot have access to legal assistance there is spiralling debt, depression, mental health problems, homelessness, criminality, family breakdown – all with knock-on costs to other public services. GPs report a large increase in the number of patients who would have been assisted by advice on benefits, employment, debts and housing.[20]

Many in the front line gave compelling evidence to the Commons Justice Committee about the hardship caused by this misguided policy. Islington Law Centre reported that two people had collapsed in its offices because of a lack of food. They had received benefits sanctions and had not contested them. In one case, a man had not eaten for six days. In the other, the woman who collapsed had three small children. She had been sanctioned for three months and was unable to feed her family.[21]

---

19 The National Audit Office found in its report that the increase in litigants in person has led to an estimated £3.4 million of additional costs for the Ministry of Justice in family courts alone. House of Commons Justice Committee, *Impact of Changes to Civil Legal Aid under Part 1 of the Legal Aid, Sentencing and Punishment of Offenders Act 2012*, 12 March 2015, Eighth Report of Session 2014-15, HC Paper 311, p. 29, §99.

20 The Ministry made estimates of the amount saved to the taxpayer by slashing legal aid – but not the knock-on costs of wasted court time or the additional costs in the public sector. *Implementing Reforms to Civil Legal Aid*, pp. 6–7, §5 and §7.

21 *Impact of Changes to Civil Legal Aid*, pp. 20–21, §49–50.

Though the reforms took family law out of the scope of legal aid, there is an exception in cases where domestic violence is alleged. Abuse victims, however, need very specific evidence of domestic violence (subject to a two year limit) to qualify, such as evidence of a stay in a refuge, a police caution, a protective injunction, or a doctor's letter. The most common form of abuse is emotional and psychological and often cannot be proved.[22]

In 2013, the Ministry of Justice set up an 'exceptional funding scheme' to provide aid to those whose human rights might be breached without it. The application process is so complicated that most people cannot use it.[23] The Legal Aid Agency received only a third of the expected number of applications in its first year. It granted funding to fewer than five per cent.[24] The Court of Appeal ruled in 2014 that the guidelines on approving funding were so strict that they breached the Convention right to a fair trial.[25]

In the 2014–15 parliamentary session, the Commons Justice Committee took evidence from those who witnessed the impact of the cuts at first hand. One couple with learning difficulties could not contest their child's adoption because they earned £35 per month more than the means-tested limit. The judge in another case involving a woman with learning difficulties said she was unable to deal with representations by the other side – and as a result, faced the possibility of never seeing her child again.[26] A

---

22 *Impact of Changes to Civil Legal Aid*, pp. 26–27, §63–64 and §66–67.
23 Even for qualified lawyers one form (CIV ECF1) took three to four hours to complete because it required a detailed explanation of the legal merits of the case. *Impact of Changes to Civil Legal Aid*, p. 17, §40.
24 Sixty-nine of 1,520 were approved. *Implementing Reforms to Civil Legal Aid*, p. 5, §4.
25 *R (Gudanaviciene) v Lord Chancellor* [2014] EWCA Civ 1622.
26 *Impact of Changes to Civil Legal Aid*, p. 14, §32.

blind Nigerian man with learning difficulties was refused funding for advice to enable him to access community care. He was incapable of looking after himself. He had survived only through small handouts from a relative and by begging. The Legal Aid Agency agreed to fund his case only after losing in the High Court.[27]

Alongside cuts in legal aid, the coalition government imposed exorbitant taxes on justice by levying fees on users of the courts. Litigants have always had to pay money up front to bring a case, to reflect the administrative costs of the court. But the increase in court fees[28] meant that for the first time ever, the Treasury would turn a profit from people seeking to enforce their legal rights. In practice the change means that the justice system is too expensive for traders, small businesses and the victims of personal injuries. Most people who need to sue for between £10,000 and £20,000 must now find five per cent of that amount up front. Some people have to choose between stumping up the fee and paying for a lawyer – so they end up without legal assistance.

When these proposals were announced, the head of the judiciary, the Lord Chief Justice of England and Wales, wrote to the Minister of Justice. He warned that the government had made 'very sweeping and . . . unduly complacent assumptions' about their likely effect on access to justice.[29] He pointed out the paucity of research evidence for the proposals. His concerns went unaddressed.

For the first time ever, the government also introduced

---

27 *Impact of Changes to Civil Legal Aid*, p. 43, §109.
28 Section 180 Anti-Social Behaviour Crime and Policing Act 2014. The aim was to generate £120 million for the Treasury.
29 Letter from the Right Honourable Lord Thomas of Cwmgiedd to the Ministry of Justice, 19 December 2014.

another tax on justice — fees in employment tribunal cases. Since July 2013, a claim for unpaid wages costs a minimum of £390. Those on a low income whose salary has not come through find that virtually impossible to pay up front. A claim for discrimination or whistleblowing costs £1,200. Within two years, the number of claims brought in tribunals had dropped by sixty per cent. For claims relating to sex discrimination and equal pay, there were eighty-three and seventy-seven per cent reductions.[30]

The screw was also turned in criminal cases. In April 2015, without public consultation or parliamentary debate, the government introduced mandatory fees to fund the criminal courts system. Anyone found guilty of a crime was automatically charged between £150 and £1,200 on top of any fines, prosecution costs or victim surcharges – regardless of their ability to pay. The charges were higher for a defendant who was convicted after pleading not guilty.

That was an encroachment on the rights of the defence. It provided a financial incentive for breadline defendants to plead guilty even when they were innocent. Petty criminals are often poor, mentally ill, homeless, addicted to drugs or alcohol. They are not reliable contributors to public funds, yet they were made criminals again when they were sent back to court charged with defaulting on a sum they could never have realistically paid.

In August 2015, a thirty-two-year-old woman stole a pack of four Mars bars worth 75p from a shop in Kidderminster. She was undergoing a benefits sanction and had not eaten for two days.

---

30 The Law Society, *Parliamentary Brief on Baroness Turner of Camden's oral question 'To ask HMG what assessment they have made of the ability of individuals who are dismissed to invoke their employment rights when they cannot afford tribunal costs'*, 25 June 2015.

She pleaded guilty and was ordered to pay a charge of £150. The same month, a destitute asylum seeker was summoned to court in Leicester for defaulting on a mandatory charge of £180. Asylum seekers are forbidden to work, so he had no legal way of earning it. The owner of a burger van who occasionally gave the man food was moved to contribute £60. The magistrate, Nigel Allcoat, offered to make up the remainder of the sum – and was immediately suspended for his intervention. He resigned in protest. More than a hundred magistrates followed suit.

The House of Lords voted in October 2015 to condemn the charges. It concluded that they undermined the principle of judicial discretion, added an artificial inducement to plead guilty and made claims for savings that cannot be substantiated.[31] The policy was finally abandoned by Grayling's successor, Michael Gove, in December 2015 – less than a year after it was introduced.[32]

Most people do not regard healthcare and law care as equally important. Successive governments have treated legal aid as the Cinderella of the welfare state, an easy target for HM Treasury's axe. Populist attacks on 'fat cat lawyers' by politicians and the media have been used as propaganda to justify the attack. Access to justice is seen as a luxury rather than a necessity underpinning our way of life.

Politicians think, probably correctly, that there are few votes to be lost in attacking legal aid and court costs. It is vital that these assaults on the justice system are reversed so that everyone, rich, not-so-rich and poor, has access to justice. Yet a government that has won power with promises of further severe cuts is unlikely to

---

31 HL Deb, 14 October 2015, vol. 765, cols. 296–309. The regret motion was carried by a majority of 32.

32 'Michael Gove scraps criminal courts charge', *Guardian*, 3 December 2015.

reverse them. The rule of law will continue to be threatened by hair-shirt economics in the new age of austerity.

When I was young at the Bar, we had a legal aid and advice system of which we could be proud. There were abuses of the system by unprincipled lawyers, but instead of tackling those effectively, government after government has burned the house to roast the pig. It will take many years to repair the damage done to the justice system by political vandalism. It will not happen any time soon.

Judicial review

Judicial review is also under sustained attack. It is the main way to challenge abuses of power by the state and public bodies. Judicial review has been used by students to question their local authority when it unreasonably denied them grants to fund their studying; by street traders when their licences were unfairly revoked; and by homeowners unlawfully refused planning permission. It made the government rethink its consultation on new nuclear power plants, when the courts found that it had not been conducted fairly.[33] It gave a remedy to peaceful protestors when police turned them away from a demonstration against the Iraq war.[34] It enabled people using vital hospital services in their neighbourhood to challenge a decision to reduce them.[35]

---

33 R (Greenpeace Ltd) v Secretary of State for Trade and Industry [2007] EWHC 311 (Admin).
34 R (Laporte) v Chief Constable of Gloucestershire Constabulary [2006] UKHL 55.
35 Trust Special Administrator Appointed to South London Healthcare NHS Trust & Anor v London Borough of Lewisham & Anor [2013] EWCA Civ 1409.

Judicial review has ancient roots. It fell into disuse in the first part of the last century, when governments used wartime powers without effective control by judges. The most notorious example arose in the *Liversidge v Anderson* case. In the 1940s, the Home Secretary, Sir John Anderson, was permitted under emergency powers to imprison anyone without trial if he had 'reasonable cause' to believe they had 'hostile associations'.[36] He used these powers to commit a Jewish businessman to prison – without giving any reason. Robert Liversidge had changed his name from Jack Perlzweig. Liversidge was represented by D. N. Pritt QC, who revealed in his autobiography *From Left to Right* that the reasons for detaining him included: 'You are suspected of having been involved in commercial frauds' and 'You are the son of a Jewish rabbi'.

In 1941, a majority of Law Lords decided that the law did not require the Home Secretary to give any reason for the detention. As long as he acted in good faith, the decision was not open to review by the courts. Lord Atkin dissented. He accused the majority of abdicating their responsibility to investigate and control the executive. He protested that reducing the requirement of reasonable cause to 'good faith' amounted to giving the Minister an uncontrolled power of imprisonment. He described the other judges as more executive-minded than the executive. He said sarcastically that he knew of only one authority to support their interpretation – Humpty Dumpty, quoted at the beginning of this chapter.

The case was not overruled until 1980.[37] But by the mid-1970s, a new generation of judges understood the need to bridle

36 *Liversidge v Anderson* [1942] AC 206 (HL). The source of the power in this case was the infamous Regulation 18B of the Defence (General) Regulations 1939.
37 *IRC v Rossminster Estates* [1980] AC 952 (HL).

arbitrary power. They breathed life into judicial review by creating a special procedure to make it work in practice. They included safeguards against abuse of the procedure, allowing cases to proceed only where the person seeking a remedy acts quickly and only if the court is satisfied it is in the interests of justice. Remedies for abuses of power are granted only where a court considers it just. It is a fair and balanced system and it did not require political interference.

Judicial review was used successfully to resist arbitrary and unjust actions by Chris Grayling's Ministry. In 2013, the coalition restricted legal aid to those who had been resident in the UK for more than twelve months.[38] In practice it meant that some of the most vulnerable groups could not seek justice – asylum seekers, victims of human trafficking, homeless people and prisoners in the custody of UK armed forces overseas. When challenged in the courts, Chris Grayling claimed that this lifeline to vindicating a legal right was 'no more than a form of social welfare or benefit'. The High Court disagreed, but was reversed by the Court of Appeal.[39]

In 2014, without parliamentary approval or debate, Chris Grayling also restricted access to legal aid in judicial review

---

38 Under section 1 of the Legal Aid, Sentencing and Punishment of Offenders Act 2012 the Lord Chancellor is obliged to make legal aid available for civil legal claims as outlined in Part 1 Schedule 1. Under section 9 the Lord Chancellor has the power to amend Part 1 Schedule 1. It was this section 9 power that Chris Grayling used to create a 12-month residency test for legal aid.

39 R (Public Law Project) v Secretary of State for Justice (Office of the Children's Commissioner intervening) [2014] EWHC 2365 (Admin), §61–88. This was overturned by the Court of Appeal [2015] EWCA Civ 1193.

cases.[40] He ordered that legal aid lawyers must not receive payment for their services unless the courts granted an application for judicial review permission to proceed. That might seem sensible – to avoid wasting taxpayer money on a pointless case. The reality, however, is that many cases denied permission are not pointless. Often the threat of judicial review proceedings alerts a public authority to its mistake – and if a public authority rectifies that mistake before the permission hearing, permission is refused and good public administration well served.

If lawyers concerned about unremunerated time and money refused to shoulder the financial risk, illegal actions would lie unchallenged. A group of solicitors' firms mounted a legal challenge against the Minister's decision. They argued successfully that Grayling had limited payments in a way that was not rationally connected with his stated purpose of giving legal aid providers incentives to undertake rigorous scrutiny of the merits of a claim.[41]

As part of a scheme to push prisoners to work towards their own rehabilitation, Grayling restricted their supply of books. He did so while admitting that reading and learning were critical to rehabilitation. The High Court ruled that the effect of the policy was contrary to its stated intention.[42]

---

40 Using his sections 1 and 9 powers under the Legal Aid, Sentencing and Punishment of Offenders Act 2012 Chris Grayling amended Regulation 5A of the Civil Legal Aid (Remuneration) Regulations 2013 (SI 2013/422).
41 R (*Ben Hoare Bell Solicitors & Ors*) v *The Lord Chancellor* [2015] EWHC 523 (Admin).
42 The policy's stated intention was to 'strengthen and support efforts to reduce reoffending and rehabilitate prisoners as well as giving the public greater confidence in the prison system'. R (*Gordon-Jones*) v *Secretary of State for Justice and The Governor of HM Prison Send* [2014] EWHC 3997

Grayling claimed that judicial review had become 'a promotional tool for countless Left-wing campaigners',[43] designed to 'force the government to change its mind over properly taken decisions by democratically elected politicians'.[44] He complained too that it was open to abuse by parties seeking 'cheap headlines'.[45] He said that the number of cases had increased too much and that it was a system that wasted court time and taxpayer money.

He produced no evidence that judges had failed to exercise their discretion properly, or that the outcome in judicial review proceedings had been against the public interest. He deplored the nearly threefold increase in the number of applications between 2000 and 2012, but that happened because other ways of bringing an appeal in immigration cases had been restricted. Once immigration cases were removed from the statistics, the number of judicial review applications had remained stable.[46]

For the government to have abridged the right of judicial review overtly would have clearly violated the rule of law and been subject to legal challenge. Grayling's tactics instead were to introduce practical hurdles to obstruct access to justice. He

---

(Admin), §9. Chris Grayling's successor, Michael Gove, wisely scrapped the policy in July 2015.

43 Chris Grayling, *Daily Mail*, 11 September 2013.

44 Chris Grayling, 'We must stop the legal aid abusers tarnishing Britain's justice system', *Telegraph*, 20 April 2014.

45 Ministry of Justice, *Judicial Review: Proposals for further reform*, Cm 8703, September 2013, p. 3.

46 Judicial reviews increased from 4,300 in 2000 to 12,600 in 2012. Immigration and asylum applications more than doubled between 2007 and 2012 and made up 76% of the total applications in 2012. Joint Committee on Human Rights, *The Implications for Access to Justice of the Government's Proposals to Reform Judicial Review*, 30 April 2014, Thirteenth Report of Session 2013–14, HL Paper 174 and HC Paper 868, p. 13, §27.

introduced a provision in the Criminal Justice and Courts Bill to force judges to deny permission on a technicality. Had it been passed in the form Grayling originally proposed, it would have meant that ministers could act outside the law as long as their illegal action had no adverse consequences for the *particular* person bringing a review. Grayling also tried to stop NGOs and public interest groups from intervening in cases, by dramatically increasing their financial burden if they did so.

Interveners generally have no direct interest in a case. They take part at the invitation of the court – because they can contribute to the consideration of a case. Amnesty International, Liberty and JUSTICE are among the many groups that bring valuable interventions. Interveners have helped to ensure that the treatment of juveniles in police custody, for example, meets international legal standards.[47] They have, for example, brought to the courts' attention the lack of coordination between housing authorities and social services across the country.[48]

Grayling treated justice as a mere commodity and not a necessity. We fought back in the Lords across the House.[49] After suffering multiple defeats in the Lords, Grayling made some

---

47 R (HC) v Secretary of State for the Home Department and Metropolitan Police [2013] EWHC 982 (Admin). The interveners in this case were the Coram Children's Legal Centre and the Howard League.

48 R (TG) v London Borough of Lambeth [2011] EWCA Civ 526. The intervener was Shelter, the charity for the homeless.

49 The Lords rejected the Criminal Justice and Courts Bill twice. On the second occasion the House approved Lord Pannick's amendments to (i) give the court discretion on whether a case was in the public interest even if it was 'highly likely' that the outcome for the individual would be the same had the public body not acted unlawfully, and (ii) that there remain no consideration of the financial resources of charities, NGOs and donors who help to fund judicial review when awarding costs. HL Deb 9 December 2014, vol. 757, cols. 1715–1752.

concessions[50] (at one stage, he had to apologise for misleading Parliament during the debates).[51] But when the Criminal Justice and Courts Act 2015 came into force, judicial review – and with it the rule of law – had been weakened. Grayling is now Leader of the House of Commons. It is unlikely that the damage will be undone by the Cameron government.

Open justice and secret trials

The principle of open justice is deep-rooted in our common law tradition. Trials must be fair but they must also be seen to be fair, or public confidence in our legal system is undermined. Exceptions to open justice must be necessary and proportionate. The press and public may be excluded from all or part of a trial to protect a vulnerable child in custody proceedings, for example, or to protect the private lives of parties, or to stop a court's orders from being thwarted. But administrative convenience and avoiding political embarrassment do not suffice to close the courtroom from public gaze.

If the way that courts behave is hidden from the public ear and eye, we lose a crucial safeguard against an unfair trial. There are other essential safeguards of fairness. Even where open justice is restricted a party must know the case against him, be

---

50 Grayling's concessions were to set a threshold amount of money provided by donors before the identity of the donor must be disclosed and to undertake a consultation on where that threshold should be set (indicating it is likely to be around £1,500). He maintained that the test must be 'exceptional public interest'. Although he conceded that the judiciary would retain the final decision on whether the test was met, he stated that judges would be required to 'formally certify and explain their reasons'. HC Deb 13 January 2015, vol. 590, cols. 808–824.

51 HC Deb 13 January 2015, vol. 590, col. 810.

presumed innocent until proven guilty and be guaranteed other rights of the defence.

National security is of first importance and the very reason for having the security and intelligence agencies. But some degree of openness and accountability is essential. The Home Office and security agencies have found it hard to accept this. They have not understood that unnecessary secrecy in the name of national security undermines public confidence in their vital work. The agencies have a better case for some protection from open justice than some liberal critics allow, but they go too far. Instead of explaining their activities, they respond to questions by refusing to confirm or deny them.

Finding a fair balance between justice and national security is difficult. The principles clashed when Karamjit Chahal was faced with deportation to India in 1990. He was an advocate of Sikh separatism, pursuing an independent homeland, Khalistan, in the province of Punjab. The Home Secretary deemed his presence in the UK to be not conducive to the public good. The British government accused him of planning terrorist attacks in the UK as well as India and of orchestrating a 'campaign of intimidation' against parts of the UK's Sikh community.

Mr Chahal denied the allegations. He was not informed of the evidence against him. He feared that if he were deported to India, he would be tortured. India's National Human Rights Commission had recorded complaints against the Punjab police involving arbitrary arrests, disappearances, and deaths in custody. Punjab security forces had assassinated suspected militants and were capable of pursuing targets into other parts of India. Key figures in the campaign had been tortured or killed or had fled overseas. India's Supreme Court had ordered investigations into police activities.

Because his case involved national security, Mr Chahal had

no right to appeal in the English courts against the decision to deport him. He was permitted only to make representations to an 'advisory panel' of senior judicial figures – without legal representation and without knowing more than an outline of the grounds for his deportation. The panel's decision was kept secret and the Home Secretary was not obliged to follow it. So Mr Chahal complained to the European Court of Human Rights.[52]

The Strasbourg Court agreed with the British government that where national security is at stake, confidential material might need to be used in a trial. But it recognised that there were better techniques for balancing national security with the individual's right to procedural justice. One was borrowed from Canada and put forward by NGOs intervening in the case. It involved a closed hearing in which a judge examined sensitive evidence. The claimant was excluded and so was his legal representative, but a security-vetted barrister – known as a 'Special Advocate' – took his place. The Special Advocate could go behind the veil of secrecy, cross-examine witnesses and test the strength of the prosecution's case.

That compromise is second-best to true equality of arms because the Special Advocate cannot take instructions from the claimant.[53] It is better than using evidence immune from any challenge at all. In a choice of evils, it is imperative to choose the least harmful.

After Karamjit Chahal's case, I was involved in a case about alleged religious or political discrimination against Republicans in Northern Ireland. They complained that they had been

---

52 *Chahal v United Kingdom* [1996] 23 EHRR 413.
53 *Al Rawi & Ors v The Security Services & Ors* [2011] UKSC 34, *per* Lord Kerr.

refused government contracts because of their religious and political beliefs. When they lodged a complaint with Northern Ireland's Fair Employment Agency, the government claimed that they had been refused the work and blacklisted on national security grounds.

The work involved access to vital power supplies and public buildings, so security vetting was appropriate. But we could not test the government's claim, because the Minister certified that key documents were immune from disclosure in the 'public interest' and his certificate was conclusive. The immunity meant the High Court of Northern Ireland could not examine whether there had been unlawful discrimination. I referred the Strasbourg Court to the Special Advocate model, to show that there were ways for the court to take account of confidential material without severely prejudicing either national security or a fair trial. The Court ruled that the national security certificates should be set aside to allow independent judicial inspection of the evidence, whether by open or closed hearing.[54] That was an important vindication of the European rule of law.

In the aftermath of these cases, Parliament created the Special Immigration Appeals Commission (SIAC). It decides appeals against the immigration authorities when they deprive someone of citizenship, or deport them on grounds of national security or the public good. SIAC has the same powers as the High Court and is presided over by senior judges – but it can and does use closed hearings and Special Advocates.

---

54 *Tinnelly & Sons v United Kingdom; McElduff v United Kingdom* (1998) 27 EHRR 249. The European Court of Justice had reached a similar conclusion in *Johnston v Chief Constable of the Royal Ulster Constabulary* [1986] ECR 1651.

But it was when the government decided to extend this procedure to civil cases involving national security that the controversy became red-hot. It led to furious political wrangling within and beyond Parliament.

It happened in this way. After the terrorist attacks on 11 September 2001, the United States established a network of secret CIA prisons in locations across the world, hidden from the reach of the US justice system. One of the most notorious was a detention camp at Guantanamo Bay, where individuals captured overseas with suspected links to al Qaeda or the Taliban were detained without trial. The Bush Administration's strategy included using what was euphemistically termed 'extraordinary rendition'. In plain language, it meant capturing someone and putting him on a plane to a prison in another country to be detained and interrogated without safeguards against arbitrary detention or torture.

On 19 January 2002, eight days after Guantanamo Bay opened as a detention facility, the US Secretary of Defense sent a memo to the Joint Chiefs of Staff. It explained that he had decided that the Taliban and al Qaeda were not entitled to prisoner of war status under the Geneva Conventions; it argued that Common Article 3 governing non-international armed conflicts did not apply to them either; and that the prisoners were to be treated according to international law only to the extent consistent with 'military necessity'.[55]

Within a year, the Secretary of Defense had authorised the Southern Commander at Guantanamo Bay to use fifteen new interrogation techniques. Camp officials were allowed to hood prisoners, to remove their clothing and comfort items (including religious items), to deprive them of light and noise, to hold

---

55 Memorandum from Donald Rumsfeld to the Chairman of the Joint Chiefs of Staff, 'Status of Taliban and Al Qaeda', 19 January 2002.

them in isolation for thirty days at a time, to interrogate them for twenty-eight hours, to force them into stress positions, to exploit their phobias, to induce stress and to deceive them with falsified documents and reports.[56]

The CIA was also authorised to carry out these so-called 'enhanced' interrogations in secret prisons around the world. Much of what took place still remains secret, though some techniques have become public. They include depriving a prisoner of sleep for eleven days at a time, confining them in a cramped space with an insect, to exploit a fear of insects; and inducing feelings of suffocation by covering a prisoner's nose and mouth with a wet towel and dripping water over it as they try to breathe[57] – known as 'waterboarding'.

Detainees alleged that the UK agencies had facilitated extraordinary rendition to these camps. Ministers denied that UK-controlled airports or airspace had been involved. It was also alleged that the agencies had given information to the US authorities for use in 'enhanced' interrogations. An All Party Parliamentary Group on Extraordinary Rendition tried to get to the truth. Revelations were slow and piecemeal. To this day, there has not been full public disclosure of what actually went on.

Matters came to a head in our courts in Binyam Mohamed's case.[58] An Ethiopian national, he had lived in the UK for several years. In 2002, he was arrested in Pakistan. He was then 'rendered'

---

56 Memorandum from William J. Haynes II to the Secretary of Defense, 'Counter-Resistance Techniques', 27 November 2002.
57 Memorandum from Steven G. Bradbury to John Rizzo, 'Interrogation of Al Qaeda Operative', 1 August 2002.
58 R (Binyam Mohamed) v Secretary of State for Foreign and Commonwealth Affairs [2010] EWCA Civ 65.

to Morocco, Afghanistan and Guantanamo, where he was imprisoned for five years. He was interrogated by US officials – with the help of information passed to them by the UK agencies.

The US authorities charged Binyam Mohamed with terrorist offences that carried the death penalty. He had made several confessions – but he claimed that he had been tortured and held incommunicado for two years without access to a lawyer. While still in Guantanamo anticipating that charges would be brought against him, he brought legal proceedings in England seeking access to information to prove that he had been tortured. The Foreign Secretary, David Miliband, refused to release it. The government did have information given to him in confidence by US authorities, but Miliband claimed that its disclosure would cause the US to lose trust in Britain, compromising their special intelligence-sharing relationship and thereby damaging the UK's national security.

The High Court looked at the evidence. It concluded that the UK agencies had facilitated wrongdoing, and that the information sought was essential to a fair consideration of Mohamed's case. To protect the intelligence-sharing relationship, however, the court deleted seven paragraphs from its published judgment. Those paragraphs summarised a confidential US government report showing that our services had known how Binyam Mohamed was being 'treated' when they facilitated his interrogation.

Binyam Mohamed's lawyers brought proceedings to make those paragraphs public. The authorities attempted to prevent public disclosure.[59] By then the United States courts had publicly

---

59 The Court ruled that disclosure was subject to any public interest immunity claim by the Foreign Secretary. The information sought by Binyam Mohamed was subsequently made available to his lawyers as a result of habeas corpus proceedings in the US, so the only outstanding issue in the English judicial review claim became whether the redacted paragraphs should be made public.

established that Binyam Mohamed had been tortured. But the Foreign Secretary gave written evidence that if the paragraphs were made public, the USA would re-evaluate its intelligence-sharing arrangement with the UK.

The Court of Appeal upheld the principles of open justice and the rule of law by ordering publication of the redacted paragraphs. This caused consternation in official circles in London and Washington DC. The State Department and the CIA apparently believed that British judges could not be trusted to protect national security. That was ludicrous: I know of no case where that criticism could fairly be made. But it was apparently the US Administration's belief and it made them determined to ensure that it would not happen again.

By this time Mohamed had been released from Guantanamo and returned to England. The authorities had dropped all charges against him. He and several other former Guantanamo detainees sued the British government for complicity in their rendition and torture. The government denied liability. It also claimed that their defence rested on material that could not be made public without harming national security. It asked the court to let them give this evidence in secret, with the detainees' interests represented by Special Advocates.

The government argued that without a closed hearing it would be forced to settle the claims, paying out large sums in compensation even though it believed it had done nothing unlawful. The case went to the Supreme Court. It ruled that extending the use of the Special Advocate procedure was a matter for Parliament, not the courts. Lord Kerr pointed out that the law's starting point is a constitutional right to be informed of the case against you. The government was asking the courts to create an entirely new exception, with no parliamentary underpinning. That made legislation inevitable.

In 2010, the Justice Secretary announced that the government had paid compensation to the Guantanamo detainees, to avoid litigation. He did not disclose the figure because the settlement was confidential. But he said that if the case had gone ahead, it would have cost the taxpayer between £30 million and £50 million. He warned that the government faced more cases of this kind. The Prime Minister, David Cameron, announced plans to extend the Special Advocate procedure to all civil cases involving issues of national security through a Justice and Security Bill.

Lawyers acting for Binyam Mohamed and civil liberties groups refused to accept the need for a closed evidence procedure. They wanted the House of Lords to block the Bill at the outset. That had little support or hope of happening but it led to resignations of high profile Liberal Democrats and recriminations against those of us who fought to improve the Bill.

In my view there was merit in legislation to allow closed evidence procedure. Just as the agencies should be entitled to defend themselves against allegations of complicity in torture, so the government should not be deterred from bringing proceedings against suspected terrorists by the risk of material, properly secret, becoming public through the trial process.[60] Open justice must sometimes give way to the need to do justice. I could support legislation if it applied only in rare, exceptional cases – to be determined by judges, not by ministers – and if it contained other effective safeguards against abuse. But the Home Office and the agencies would have none of it. Their proposals put ministers rather than judges in charge of the decision to hold a hearing in secret.

---

60 *Guardian News Media & Ors v Incedal* [2014] EWCA Crim 1861, §14–17.

The Justice and Security Bill empowered ministers to decide whether trials should be held in secret. Parliament's Joint Committee on Human Rights described it as a radical departure from the UK's tradition of open justice and fairness.[61] The Lords removed many of the more troubling clauses. The Commons accepted most of our changes, including the requirement that judges have the final say on whether to use the procedure. Yet secret courts are still second-best to true equality between the parties. They are a compromise that the rule of law can withstand only if carefully controlled by the courts.[62]

Unfinished business

There is other unfinished business in protecting the European rule of law. The Strasbourg Court urgently needs additional funds to enable it to clear the crippling backlog of pending cases. It used to tackle the problem by dumping cases on an industrial scale using a single judge to strike them out without giving reasons. That was unfair and undermined public confidence. It has promised that in future the judge will have to give reasons

---

61 Joint Committee on Human Rights (JCHR), *Legislative Scrutiny: Justice and Security Bill*, 13 November 2012, Fourth Report of Session 2012–13, HL Paper 59 and HC Paper 370, p. 3. I was a founding member of the JCHR and served on the Committee from July 2001 to March 2015.

62 Worryingly, government statistics give early signs that applications for closed hearings are becoming 'the norm' in security sensitive cases. From 2013–14 – the first year after the Act came into being – there were five official applications for closed hearings. A year later that figure had more than doubled, to 11. Source: Use of closed material procedure report: 25 June 2014 to 24 June 2015, presented to Parliament pursuant to section 12 of the Justice and Security Act 2013 in October 2015.

for rejecting a case – but it remains to be seen whether they will be sufficiently detailed to satisfy what the rule of law requires.

There have been other improvements in the way the Strasbourg system works, but reforms are needed at national level. It is essential to ensure that candidates for judicial office in both European Courts are of high quality. In the recent past it has been near impossible to persuade UK judges to apply. They do not need to be serving judges but they do need to have sufficient knowledge and experience to make an effective contribution. The common law system has many benefits and we must recognise the contribution made by British judges when they return from serving in Europe.

Other European nations are watching to see whether the government follows through on Conservative threats to treat rulings by the Strasbourg Court as advisory rather than binding. The Secretary General of the Council of Europe has urged the UK government not to endanger freedoms in Ukraine, Russia and elsewhere by undermining the authority of judges in Strasbourg. He said that the UK's failure to implement the prisoner voting case was the first example of a Council of Europe member openly refusing to implement a judgment – and warned of the danger that other governments would follow the UK's lead.[63] His concern is well founded.

Instead of flouting the Court's binding judgments on prisoner voting and threatening to decouple the British system from the European Convention on Human Rights, the government should welcome the dialogue that now occurs between our Supreme Court and Strasbourg. Instead of attacking the Strasbourg Court for overreaching itself, British politicians and

---

63 'Tories urged to show caution on European human rights', *Financial Times*, 16 October 2015.

the British press should press the government to comply with its judgments against the UK, in accordance with our international legal obligations. Instead of rewriting the Ministerial Code to remove reference to the UK's overarching duty to obey international law, the government should seek to strengthen the powers of the Committee of Ministers of the Council of Europe to tackle repeated and systemic violations of the Convention, including by means of financial penalties.

Realpolitik abounds. There is no doubt about the urgency of what is at stake – nothing less than the survival of a viable system which maintains the confidence of those it was designed to protect.

Then there is the international system of human rights protection. If the Commonwealth means anything it is in protecting and upholding the rule of law. But there is little enthusiasm across the Commonwealth to translate rhetoric into reality. The UN Human Rights Council is split by divisions between Muslim and secular countries. The human rights treaty bodies monitor discrimination on the basis of gender, race and disability.[64] They protect vulnerable groups including children, migrant workers and the victims of enforced disappearances. But they are underfunded, and governments – including our own – too often ignore their opinions or pay lip service to them. Successive UK

---

64 The treaty bodies are: the UN Human Rights Committee, the UN Committee on Economic, Social and Cultural Rights, the UN Committee for the Elimination of Racial Discrimination, the UN Committee for the Elimination of Discrimination Against Women, the UN Committee Against Torture, the UN Committee on the Rights of the Child, the UN Committee on the Rights of Persons with Disabilities, the UN Committee on Enforced Disappearances and the UN Committee on Migrant Workers.

governments have refused to allow complaints against them to be taken to the UN Human Rights Committee. The current UN High Commissioner for Human Rights, Zeid Ra'ad Al Hussein, is impressive but his office is pitifully starved of resources.

Civil society – led by international NGOs such as Human Rights Watch, the Open Society Institute and Amnesty International – presses for reform in Europe, the Commonwealth and the UN. But protecting the rule of law and human rights is not high on government agendas. There is no political appetite to strengthen the ability of courts to call their governments to account, or to improve access to justice.

What matters now

The rule of law is under threat across the world. At home, we must fight to reverse the harm inflicted on a legal aid system of which we were once proud. We must restore effective access to justice for all by abolishing the need to pay exorbitant sums for court and tribunal expenses and remove unnecessary fetters on judicial review. It is wrong to charge litigants rather than taxpayers for running the justice system. It is iniquitous to impose court user fees on those who are vulnerable and disadvantaged. It is unconstitutional for an executive-dominated Parliament to restrict judicial review of the way it exercises its public powers. Secret courts must be used sparingly and effective safeguards against abuse are crucial. And in a kingdom of asymmetrical and botched devolution, it is urgent that the Ministry of Justice takes on oversight of the constitution as a whole.

The rule of law is an elusive concept. It is a force that unifies equal rights campaigns, a standard-bearer for lawmakers, a guarantor for litigants, the guard of judicial impartiality. It is an ideal we must cherish, protect, aspire to and strive for. Our government and Parliament have eroded it – and they have done so at our peril.

THE FIGHT AHEAD

A great American judge once said of the nobility of the profession of law that one may wear out one's heart striving after the unattainable.[1] Over the last fifty years what seemed unattainable became politically possible – a Human Rights Act, an Equality Act, a Civil Partnership Act, an Equal Marriage Act, a Freedom of Information Act, a Defamation Act and a Forced Marriage Act. Thanks to a new generation of judges who refuse to be timorous when faced with abuses of state power, there have also been major gains in the courts.

The legal process can and should be used as an instrument of social transformation. But the role of a reforming advocate is limited to acting for a particular client in a particular case. While the outcome of that case may promote wider change, that is not the advocate's professional role. Barristers cannot choose which case to take. Our professional code requires us to act like a London taxicab and serve all comers. When we are given an opportunity to promote reform, our role is also limited by the

---

1 Oliver Wendell Holmes Jr.

proper reluctance of judges to act as lawmakers. Judges intervene only in extreme cases of injustice, where Parliament has consistently failed to address the problem.

The role of a parliamentary advocate is also limited – by the conservatism and timidity of politicians and their advisers. Roy Jenkins was exceptional during the two liberal interludes in which he ran the Home Office. It was as his special adviser in the mid-1970s that I learned the art of the politically possible. More than any minister in my lifetime, Jenkins was willing to take large risks with his political career to act in accordance with his principles. I watched him fight against racist bigotry, against oppression of gay people, for free speech, for equality of opportunity and for Britain to remain in Europe.

The Westminster political system has been decaying for decades. Many MPs have little practical experience or hinterland beyond politics and public relations. The civil service is enfeebled – understaffed and overburdened. Many special advisers are embryonic MPs. They have too much influence and have weakened the crucial role of civil servants in challenging ministers to think and think again before they act.

Alienation from politics is widespread. Disaffection with Westminster politics is not confined to Scotland. Successive governments have failed to address the causes of popular discontent. The unity of the UK is threatened by nationalism and xenophobia and the absence of a stable constitutional framework. Our leaders speak of 'British values' as though free speech, tolerance and democracy were unique to this country. They praise free speech while seeking to ban the expression of views they dislike.

The coalition government undermined the rule of law with savage cuts to legal aid and the imposition of extortionate fees for access to the courts. It weakened equality law and the agency that is meant to enforce it. In the name of counter-terrorism it rushed through emergency legislation that harmed our privacy and lacked proper safeguards. In the wake of the Leveson report, together with Labour it persuaded Parliament to impose a state-backed system of regulation that threatens freedom of the press and free speech.

Each day David Cameron's government gives us a master class in public relations. Spin doctors hide the lack of a coherent strategy to tackle the huge problems facing this country and beyond. The Prime Minister plays with populist English nationalism and defers to corporate interests to safeguard his political survival as Conservative leader – of a party divided by different degrees of hostility to Europe. His is a reactionary government. Unless it collapses it will be in office for five long years.

The Prime Minister now wishes to pull back the Freedom of Information Act, obscuring our right to know what politicians do in our name. The threats to the Human Rights Act and the European human rights system menace the victims of government oppression, who may yet lose their right to obtain redress. Other important issues are being sidelined. The rejection by MPs of attempts to permit doctor-assisted suicide makes reform unlikely in the lifetime of this Parliament. It is also unlikely that women and girls in Northern Ireland will soon have access to safe abortions.

European governments fail to act together in responding to the humanitarian crisis of mass migration. We need and we lack European institutions able and willing to tackle this and other problems that cannot be solved by any one country on its own: terrorism and other serious crimes, gross violations of human dignity, threats to the environment, health and welfare. Top-heavy European bureaucracies are in need of drastic surgery. And governments need to provide sufficient resources to enable the overburdened European Court of Human Rights to deal fairly and efficiently with complaints of violations of fundamental rights and freedoms.

The achievements of the past fifty years now stand seriously threatened. There is much to defend and fortify and undo – and so much need for your active involvement in the pursuit of justice. Now over to you.

INDEX

References to footnotes are indicated by n.

241